COMBAT AIRCRAFT

161 **JUNKERS Ju 88C DAY AND NIGHTFIGHTERS**

SERIES EDITOR TONY HOLMES

161

COMBAT AIRCRAFT

Chris Goss

JUNKERS Ju 88C DAY AND NIGHTFIGHTERS

OSPREY
PUBLISHING

OSPREY PUBLISHING

Bloomsbury Publishing Plc

Kemp House, Chawley Park, Cumnor Hill, Oxford, OX2 9PH, UK

Bloomsbury Publishing Ireland Limited,

29 Earlsfort Terrace, Dublin 2, D02 AY28, Ireland

1359 Broadway, 12th Floor, New York, NY 10018, USA

E-mail; info@ospreypublishing.com

www.ospreypublishing.com

OSPREY is a trademark of Osprey Publishing Ltd

First published in Great Britain in 2026

A catalogue record for this book is available from the British Library.

ISBN: PB 9781472867872; eBook 9781472867896; ePDF 9781472867889; XML 9781472867865

26 27 28 29 30   10 9 8 7 6 5 4 3 2 1

Edited by Tony Holmes
Cover Artwork by Gareth Hector
Aircraft Profiles by Janusz Światłoń
Index by Richard Munro
Typeset by Lumina Datamatics Ltd
Printed by Repro India Ltd

Osprey Publishing supports the Woodland Trust, the UK's leading woodland conservation charity.

To find out more about our authors and books visit **www.ospreypublishing.com**. Here you will find extracts, author interviews, details of forthcoming events and the option to sign up for our newsletter.

For product safety related questions contact productsafety@bloomsbury.com

Front Cover

At the outbreak of War, Leutnant Manfred Riegel was the *Gruppenadjutant* of the Bf 110 unit I./ZG 76. On 21 February 1940, he joined newly formed Z./KG 30 and then flew the Ju 88C-1 and C-2 operationally throughout the campaign in Norway. During the late afternoon of 25 April 1940, he was flying one of four Ju 88C-1s of Z./KG 30, which, along with an unknown number of Bf 110s from I./ZG 76, were escorting Ju 88As of 2./KG 30 in a bombing raid in the Dombås/Åandalsnes area.

At 1730 hrs, Riegel strafed the frozen lake at Lesjaskog that was being used by Gladiators and Sea Gladiators of the RAF's No 263 Sqn. He was credited with the destruction of three Gloster biplane fighters on the Lake, while his Bordschütze, Obergefreiter Heinz Richard, got a fourth. Eighteen Gladiators had flown in from the carrier HMS *Glorious* the previous day, and following Riegel's attack and others made earlier in the day, only five remained serviceable by the evening of 25 April. These aircraft were evacuated to a temporary landing strip at Setnesmoen later that same evening (*Cover artwork by Gareth Hector*)

Previous Pages

A *Schwarm* of Ju 88Cs of 14./KG 40 taxi out at an airfield in western France (probably Lorient, but also possibly Bordeaux-Mérignac) for another mission over the Bay of Biscay in the summer of 1943. The aircraft in the foreground has been painted in the unit's unique lighter grey camouflage, which was increasingly applied to aircraft rather than the two-tone green scheme due to its greater effectiveness during overwater operations (*Author's Collection*)

CONTENTS

INTRODUCTION

With the Luftwaffe buoyed by the Ju 88A-1's performance when it first saw action as a bomber in October 1939 with I. *Gruppe* of *Kampfgeschwader* 30 (I./KG 30), a fighter version soon appeared on the Junkers production line. The Ju 88 V7 prototype fighter had first flown in September 1938, and this resulted in the production of 20 Ju 88C-1s. This twin-engined fighter was essentially a converted Ju 88A-1 powered by Junkers Jumo 211B engines that featured a solid nose, rather than the distinctive glazed nose of the bomber. The modified nose section housed a single 20 mm MG 151 or MG FF cannon and three 7.92 mm MG 17 machine guns, all of which were mounted forward of an 11 mm armoured bulkhead. It could also carry a small bomb load.

Being a fighter, the crew reduced from four to three – Flugzeugführer (pilot), Bordfunker (radio operator) and Bordschütze (gunner). Of note, the first prototype C-1, Wk-Nr 0096 (coded CN+NR), had false panelling painted onto its nose to make it look like a Ju 88A-1.

With a maximum speed of more than 500 km/h, the Ju 88C-1 was comparable with the only other German *Zerstörer* at that time, the Messerschmitt Bf 110. However, the Ju 88C-1 had a range of more than 2250 km with internal fuel, compared to the Bf 110's of around 900 km. To increase its range, the Bf 110 required either a fixed ventral tank and/or two underwing drop tanks, all of which had a detrimental effect on the aircraft's combat performance.

A Junkers factory photograph of the first prototype Ju 88C-1, Wk-Nr 0096 CN+NR, looking almost identical to a Ju 88A-1 thanks to its false glazed nose (*Author's collection*)

The definitive armament layout for the Ju 88C-6, featuring a solid nose and ventral gondola, is clearly visible in this close-up of an aircraft from 10./ZG 26. This unit flew escort and daylight intercept missions with the aircraft in the Mediterranean in 1942–44 (*Author's collection*)

Four months after the Ju 88A-1's operational debut, a new unit was formed equipped with the Ju 88C-1. Over the years that followed, the Ju 88C-1, C-2, C-4 and C-6 would see combat operations over Norway, Britain, the Atlantic, North Africa, the Mediterranean, the Soviet Union and mainland northwest Europe by day and night as an intruder, nightfighter, heavy day fighter and train-buster.

Ju 88C VARIANTS

Ju 88C-1 – 20 aircraft converted from Ju 88A-1 and delivered February–April 1940. Powered by Jumo 211B-1 engines. Armed with one MG 151 or MG FF cannon and three MG 17 machine guns (all forward-firing), one MG 15 (rear-firing) and a 500 kg bomb load carried internally.

Ju 88C-2 – 20 aircraft converted from Ju 88A-5 (enlarged wingspan) or Ju 88C-1 and delivered April–September 1940, with an additional 20 delivered date unknown. Powered by Jumo 211B-1 engines. Armed with one MG 151 or MG FF/M cannon and three MG 17 machine guns (all forward-firing), one MG 15 (rear-firing) and a 500 kg bomb load carried internally.

Ju 88C-4 – based on Ju 88A-4 (enlarged wingspan), 60 built/converted from Ju 88A-5 and delivered September 1940–April 1941. Powered by Jumo 211B-1 engines. Armed with one MG 151 or MG FF/M cannon and three MG 17 machine guns (all forward-firing), one MG 15 (rear-firing) and a 500 kg bomb load carried internally.

Ju 88C-6 – around 900 built, based on Ju 88A-4. First 17 Ju 88C-6/B (short range) then Ju 88C-6/C became standard. Powered by Jumo 211F/J engines. Armed with three MG FF/M cannon and three MG 17, two MG 131 or two/three MG 81 machine guns (all forward-firing) and one MG 81Z (rear-firing).

Note – single Ju 88C-3 converted from Ju 88A-5 Wk-Nr 0367 which became single Ju 88C-5 (with BMW 801 engines and no forward-firing cannon) and then the first of four Ju 88C-7s (fast strategic reconnaissance).

CHAPTER ONE

Z.St./KG 30

From February 1940, the first and, as it would transpire, only batch of 20 Ju 88C-1s (sometimes known as the Ju 88Z) were available for operational testing. A new unit was formed on 21 February to evaluate these aircraft. The only fully operational Ju 88 *Kampfgeschwader* at that time was KG 30, so it was decided to form *Zerstörer Staffel* (Z.St.)/KG 30. The *Staffel*, based at Perleberg, was subordinate to Hauptmann Fritz Doensch's I./KG 30 as well as to the main Ju 88 training unit *Ergänzungsgruppe* 4, formerly *Lehrgruppe* Ju 88, commanded by Major Friedrich-Karl Knust.

Command of Z.St./KG 30 went to 27-year-old Oberleutnant Herbert Bönsch, while other pilots were posted in mainly from Bf 110 units. Amongst those sent to Perleberg were Unteroffiziere Albrecht Weimann and Heinz Strüning from 5./*Zerstörergeschwader* (ZG) 26 and Leutnant Manfred Riegel from *Stab* I./ZG 76. Initially, the *Staffel* was expected to have 13 crews and 15 aircraft, but the first Ju 88s did not arrive until around the middle of March, and by 9 April – the start of the German invasion of Norway – it had 12 crews and just six aircraft based at Perleberg, but neither had yet been declared fully combat ready.

Training was not without incident. On the evening of 31 March, Oberleutnant Gerhard Freiherr Grote was killed in an accident at Greifswald, with Unteroffizier Walter Zugst passing away in hospital the following day. However, it is believed that due to a lack of Ju 88s on strength, the crash possibly involved a Do 17M-1.

At the end of the Norway campaign, Z.St./KG 30 became 4./NJG 1. Aircraft in this photograph show a mixture of KG 30 markings (4D code) and the *Kampfgeschwader*'s diving eagle insignia on their noses, but with the black-painted aircraft carrying the markings of 4./NJG 1 (CM and FM codes) (*Simon Schatz*)

With the distance from Germany to Norway and, as it would transpire, distances of missions within Norway itself, the only fighters capable of long range escort were the Bf 110s and the newly arrived Ju 88C-1s. Therefore, for the Norwegian campaign, it was decided that Z.St./KG 30 would work alongside the Bf 110s of Hauptmann Günther Reinecke's I./ZG 76, but still remain subordinate to I./KG 30. All three units initially flew from Westerland and then Stavanger Sola from 10 April.

On 12 April, 36 Wellingtons, 24 Hampdens and 23 Blenheims were tasked with attacking German shipping off Stavanger throughout the day. As a result, six Hampdens and three Wellingtons were lost. The Hampdens, attacked earlier in the day, were downed by Bf 109s from II. *Gruppe* of *Jagdgeschwader* (JG) 77, which claimed eight. The Wellingtons (of Nos 38 and 149 Sqns) were intercepted by I./ZG 76 and Z.St./KG 30, with Leutnant Helmut Woltersdorf, Oberleutnant Heinz Gresens and Feldwebel Leo Schumacher of 2./ZG 76 and Oberfeldwebel Georg Fleischmann of 3./ZG 76 being credited with five Wellingtons (Woltersdorf claimed two) downed southwest of Stavanger between 1651–1735 hrs. Oberfeldwebel Martin Jeschke and Unteroffizier Peters Laufs of Z.St./KG 30 claimed two more at 1645 hrs and 1650 hrs, respectively.

Sqn Ldr Maurice Nolan of No 38 Sqn reported being under attack by enemy fighters and that his bomber was about to crash in the sea, whilst Sgts Horace Wheller and Sgt Geoff Goad of No 149 Sqn made it as far as the Norwegian coast in their aircraft, the latter last being seen at 1610 hrs with a Bf 110 in pursuit. All three Wellingtons failed to return, and there were no survivors. A number of other bombers from Nos 38 and 149 Sqns were slightly damaged, while two crews from the latter unit claimed to have shot down two Bf 110s. None were lost, however, although a Ju 88C-1 believed to have been flown by Leutnant Paul Semrau was damaged, force-landing back at Stavanger. Finally, Ju 88C-1 Wk-Nr 0136, with Unteroffizier Erich Maus at the controls, crashed whilst coming in to land at Stavanger after combat. Maus, Bordfunker Gefreiter Michael Hoch and Bordschütze Flieger Hans Rack all perished.

Unteroffizier Heinz Strüning's Ju 88C-1 Wk-Nr 0142 4D+MH trails smoke after being hit by Swedish anti-aircraft fire on 7 June 1940, the fighter being engaged after straying over the neutral country. Despite serious damage to his port engine, Strüning managed to successfully crash-land the Ju 88C-1 at Bjørnfjell, on the Swedish border, although the aircraft was wrecked in the process (*Author's collection*)

On 13 April, both Z.St./KG 30 and I./ZG 76 were credited with downing Hudsons, Ju 88C pilot Unteroffizier Peters Laufs making the first of these claims following an encounter with RAF aircraft east of Stavanger at 1115 hrs. This was followed by Leutnant Helmut Fahlbusch of 3./ZG 76 at 1352 hrs and Unteroffizier Ulrich Brückner of 1./ZG 76 at 1725 hrs. Two aircraft from No 220 Sqn reported being attacked off Stavanger by what they thought were Bf 110s at 0940 hrs and 1005 hrs. In the first engagement, the Hudson flown by South African Flt Lt Harry Sheahan was damaged and the unidentified turret gunner wounded, although the latter claimed to have damaged his attacker. The crew of the second aircraft, flown by Flg Off Murray Petrie (who who would be killed in action 11 days later), recorded an inconclusive combat. These times match with Laufs' victory claims.

Two No 233 Sqn Hudsons were lost later in the day, and they match the I./ZG 76 claims. No German aircraft were lost or damaged in any of these combats.

The days that followed were quieter, which was a good thing for Z.St./KG 30 as on 16 April it reported having just two aircraft serviceable, five unserviceable and seven crews combat ready. The next combat did not occur until 0535 hrs on 17 April when Oberfeldwebel Martin Jeschke claimed his second victim, a Blenheim east of Stavanger at 0535 hrs. Although no Blenheims were in fact active until later in the day, Flg Off Goronwy 'Gron' Edwards, flying a Hudson of No 233 Sqn, reported his aircraft being slightly damaged by a Ju 88 in the Stavanger area. Edwards' brief account of the action read as follows;

'One enemy aircraft (Ju 88) attacked aircraft at Stavanger at 0445 hrs. Rear Gunner replied with 450 rounds which appeared to hit enemy aircraft which broke off attack at 0505 hrs.'

Later that same day Stavanger was attacked by Blenheims of No 107 Sqn and a Ju 88C-1 (believed to be Wk-Nr 0131 coded 4D+EH) destroyed.

Although I./ZG 76 remained active, claiming nine aircraft destroyed through to the end of April (and suffering the loss of *Gruppenkommandeur* Hauptmann Günther Reinecke and two other crews on the final day of the month), things were much quieter for Z.St./KG 30. This allowed the *Staffel* to declare seven crews and seven aircraft available at Trondheim on 30 April, the unit having moved to its new base on or around the 17th.

At 1730 hrs on 25 April, Z.St./KG 30 attacked parked Gladiators of No 263 Sqn on the frozen Lake Lesjaskog. Leutnant Manfred Riegel was credited with the destruction of three Gladiators and Obergefreiter Heinz Richard, Riegel's Bordschütze, one more. By now, air operations were taking place further to the north of Norway, and Z.St./KG 30's ability to carry out long-range escort for bombers made the Ju 88C-1 a highly valuable asset, albeit a limited one due to the modest number of aircraft and crews available. For example, on 17 May, the *Staffel* recorded just four aircraft serviceable, one unserviceable and five crews ready to fly.

Exactly one week earlier, the *Staffel* had lost another crew when, during an escort mission to Narvik that evening, Unteroffizier Albrecht Weimann's Ju 88C-1 Wk-Nr 0133 4D+FH suffered engine failure on the return flight and the pilot force-landed on a mountain at Storfjellet in the municipality of Bindal. All three crew were captured and quickly shipped off to Scotland. Their aircraft was relatively intact, and it was recovered in 1990 by the Royal

Norwegian Air Force and is now on display in an unrestored condition in the Norwegian Armed Forces Aircraft Collection at Gardermoen.

By the middle of May 1940, the scene of battle had moved to Narvik, with I./ZG 76 sending a *Sonderstaffel* of experienced crews led by new *Gruppenkommandeur* Hauptmann Werner Restemeyer to operate with Z.St./KG 30 from Trondheim on the 18th. While there, Restemeyer had operational control of Z.St./KG 30. Two days before his arrival, the Ju 88C-equipped *Staffel* had claimed its last aircraft in combat.

The first victory that day was recorded by Oberleutnant Herbert Bönsch when he claimed a Fleet Air Arm Roc fighter ten kilometres north of Narvik at 1300 hrs on 16 May 1940. This was in fact a Skua dive-bomber of 803 Naval Air Squadron flown by Lt Leslie Harris, with Lt John Vereker as his observer. Harris subsequently stated in his combat report;

'Combat over Narvik. With PO Glover attacked five Ju 88s, one shot down. After about six head-on attacks [I] was hit by explosive bullet in left shoulder. Force-landed Ofoten Fjord and picked up by HMS *Matabele*. PO Glover returned safely.'

No Ju 88s from Z.St./KG 30 were lost. The sighting of warships by the Luftwaffe led to a further engagement in the afternoon when Sub Lt Ian Easton and Midshipman Arthur Griffiths each claimed a Ju 88 destroyed in a combat between 1445–1500 hrs. Unteroffizier Peter Laufs claimed two Skuas in return, but these cannot be matched with any British loss.

Z.St./KG 30's total of victories would remain at seven in the air and four on the ground during the Norwegian campaign, as from now on the unit flew exclusively escort or ground suppression missions. For example, on 20 May, Ju 88C-1 Wk-Nr 0137 4D+GH, flown by Feldwebel Eugen Kretzschmer, escorted Ju 52/3ms on a supply drop to Narvik, after which

Strüning's Ju 88C-1 after its crash-landing on 7 June 1940, the wreckage being examined by personnel from the Luftwaffe and Kriegsmarine. With his aircraft rapidly losing height due to its damaged engine, it took all of Strüning's skill as a pilot to make it back into Norwegian airspace before setting the Ju 88C-1 down just west of the Swedish border. The German words scrawled on the canopy glazing translate to 'Mortal Danger', warning those looking over the fighter that its guns and ammunition have yet to be removed (*Author's collection*)

he attacked a gun position. The latter succeeded in hitting the aircraft's fuel tanks, and on the way back to Trondheim, Kretzschmer crash-landed at Vik. He and his Bordfunker Gefreiter Konstantin Erhard were captured, but Bordschütze Obergefreiter Fritz Vogt managed to escape and was back safely in German hands by 10 June.

Z.St./KG 30's final loss in Norway came on 7 June when Ju 88C-1 Wk-Nr 0142 4D+MH was hit by Swedish anti-aircraft fire and force-landed at Bjørnfjell. The pilot, believed to be Unteroffizier Heinz Strüning, and his crew were uninjured.

Narvik was captured on 8 June, and on the 16th Z.St./KG 30 returned to Düsseldorf. It was by then reporting an establishment of 15 crews and 14 aircraft, but soon after its C-1s were replaced by Ju 88C-2s. The latter were virtually identical to the C-1s, but with longer wings. The last reported C-1 loss was Wk-Nr 0126 4D+PZ, which crashed at Karstädt on 5 July, killing Flugzeugführer Unteroffizier Michael Wurm, with Obergefreiter Otto Klopp and Gefreiter Johannes Musfeld injured.

By now Z.St./KG 30 had become 4. *Staffel* of *Nachtjagdgeschwader* (NJG) 1 (the change taking effect from 1 July 1940), and in September 1940 – while still commanded by Oberleutnant Herbert Bönsch – it became 1./NJG 2. The unit soon began flying intruder missions over Britain with the Ju 88C-2 and then the C-4, the latter being a converted Ju 88A-5 with Jumo 211C/G engines and longer wings.

Amongst the pilots to see action in the Ju 88C in Norway and over Britain was Leutnant Manfred Riegel, who explained post-war;

'The *Zerstörer* version of the Ju 88 answered the expectations in a remarkable way. Its range was sufficient, the aeroplane could operate in every weather condition and it was also equal to enemy fighters of that time. I can remember a dogfight with a Hurricane near Narvik – the Hurricane was not able to outmanoeuvre the Ju 88 and soon disappeared after it had been fired on. However, it was not advisable to attack warships because their defensive armament was too heavy and they opened fire as soon as an aeroplane came near. Here too the Ju 88's handling was important.

'I found the Ju 88C-2 completely satisfactory. As soon as you sat down in the pilot's seat, you felt at home. The offensive and defensive armament, the intercom with my crew and the radio communication with the ground gave confidence. Furthermore, its characteristics, especially when flying on instruments, were outstanding.'

It is not surprising that the future for the Ju 88 as a fighter looked promising

A number of Z.St./KG 30 pilots subsequently experienced success afterwards. Herbert Bönsch would shoot down 11 aircraft at night to go with his single daylight claim. He would be awarded the German Cross in Gold prior to being killed in action on the night of 1 August 1942. By then commanding III./NJG 2, Bönsch was posthumously promoted to Major.

Leutnant Wilhelm Pack, who suffered a number of minor accidents with Z.St./KG 30, was one of the first German nightfighter pilots to shoot down an RAF bomber with 3./NJG 1. Immediately after claiming the Wellington of No 99 Sqn, flown by Plt Off Bruce Power, at 0114 hrs on 26 July 1940, his Bf 110 was shot down by return fire from another Wellington and he and his Bordfunker were killed.

Hauptmann Heinz Strüning joined the Luftwaffe in 1935, and upon the outbreak of war he was flying Bf 110s with 5./ZG 26. Following his time with Z.St./KG 30, he served with 1./NJG 2 on intruder missions over Britain. Strüning subsequently flew with 7. and 4. *Staffeln* of NJG 2, and by April 1943, when he joined 2./NJG 1, he had been awarded the Knight's Cross. Made *Staffelkapitän* of 3./NJG 1, he was awarded the Oak Leaves in July 1944, having shot down 56 aircraft. Strüning was killed in action on the night of 24 December 1944 leading 9./NJG 1, his Bf 110G being shot down by a Mosquito intruder from No 157 Sqn near Bergisch Gladbach (*Author's collection*)

Having attained the rank of Major, Paul Semrau had claimed 46 night victories prior to his death in action on 8 February 1945 while commanding II./NJG 2. He was posthumously awarded the Oak Leaves to the Knight's Cross he had received in October 1942.

Unteroffizier Heinz Strüning would shoot down 56 aircraft, and also be awarded the Oak Leaves to the Knight's Cross prior to being shot down and killed by fellow ace Flt Lt Robert 'Dolly' Doleman in a Mosquito of No 157 Sqn on Christmas Eve 1944 while commanding 9./NJG 1 with the rank of Hauptmann.

Unteroffizier Peter Laufs would shoot down a total of 12 aircraft prior to being killed in action on 27 January 1942 whilst still with 1./NJG 2. By then a Leutnant, he received the German Cross of Gold posthumously.

Rising star Oberfeldwebel Kurt Herrmann would go on to shoot down nine aircraft and be commissioned prior to his aircraft suffering engine failure on a mission over Britain on 10 March 1941 – his Ju 88 was possibly damaged by a Hurricane. Having successfully force-landed, Herrmann and his crew were captured.

Finally, Leutnant Manfred Riegel would be posted as *Gruppenadjutant* to I./NJG 2 at the end of July 1940, after which he joined *Stab.*/NJG 1 in February 1941. Although he would continue to serve as a nightfighter pilot until August 1943, Riegel failed to achieve any more victories.

CHAPTER TWO

INTRUDING OVER BRITAIN

I n June 1940, Major Wolfgang Falck, *Gruppenkommandeur* of I./ZG 1, was tasked with forming a nightfighter unit for defence of the Reich. The preferred aircraft for the role were the Bf 110C/D and Ju 88C-2. In August 1940, II./NJG 1 was duly created, commanded by Major Karl-Heinrich Heyse, an experienced bomber pilot who had fought in Spain and had led He 111-equipped 2./KG 55 until the end of January 1940.

Two of II./NJG 1's *Staffeln* would operate Ju 88C-2s and C-4s, with 4. *Staffel* being led by Oberleutnant Herbert Bönsch, formerly of Z.St/KG 30, and 6. *Staffel* led by Oberleutnant Karl Hülshoff, formerly *Staffelkapitän* of 7./KG 54 (experienced blind flying crews from III./KG 54 formed the nucleus of 6./NJG 1). II./NJG 1's 5. *Staffel* was equipped with Do 17Z-7s and Z-10s (until converting to the Ju 88 from May 1941 onwards) and commanded by Hauptmann Rolf Jung.

On 17 July 1940, Oberst Josef Kammhuber, former *Kommodore* of KG 51, was given command of the new 1. *Nachtjagddivision*. He firmly believed that suitably converted bombers such as the Do 17Z and Ju 88 flown by experienced crews would be ideal for *Fernnachtjagd* (long-range nightfighter) missions over Britain, later stating that, 'When I want to kill wasps, I smoke out their nest. I don't swat insects in the air one at a time, I go to the nest when they are in!' As a result, II./NJG 1 began intruder operations over British airfields from Gilze-Rijen, in the Netherlands.

A Ju 88C-2 or C-4 of 4./NJG 2 flies in close formation with another aircraft from the unit in late 1941. 4. *Staffel* undertook night intruder 'missions' with I./NJG 2 over both Britain and the Mediterranean (*Author's collection*)

The first reported claims came on the night of 23 July when Feldwebeln Otto Wiese and Gustav Schramm of 4. *Staffel* each claimed what they thought were Wellingtons over the North Sea. The only aircraft reported lost that night was in fact a Blenheim of No 110 Sqn flown by Sgt Cliff Heyward, which crashed off Haamstede, in the Netherlands.

However, Wellington crews from Nos 9 and 149 Sqns reported being attacked by Bf 110s, with the aircraft from the latter unit, flown by Plt Off George Panter, being targeted on its outward journey 60 miles off the English coast at around the time the German claims were made. Observer, Plt Off Robert Sterling, was killed and the aircraft forced to return to base, landing at 2255 hrs.

The next claim came on the night of 17–18 August, when Feldwebel Peter Laufs, formerly of Z.St./KG 30 and now flying with 4./NJG 1, claimed a Hurricane off Lowestoft, in Suffolk, the identity of which has never been confirmed. Some Luftwaffe records state he was in a Bf 110 during this combat. Later that same night, a Ju 88C-2 of 4./NJG 1 flown by Oberfeldwebel Fritz Zenkel was reported missing over the North Sea. It has been suggested that he fell victim to a No 29 Sqn Blenheim IF flown by Plt Off Richard Rhodes (who would be killed in action along with the rest of his three-man crew exactly one week later). He claimed to have engaged what he thought was an He 111 ten miles south of Chester, in Cheshire, at 0228 hrs, finally shooting it down into the sea east of Spurn Head, off the coast of the East Riding of Yorkshire, at 0320 hrs.

Rhodes' initial interception would have been too far west for a *Fernnachtjäger* to have been operating, but a Wellington flown by Flg Off Alban Hough of No 37 Sqn reported a combat with what his crew thought was a Bf 110 40 miles east of Great Yarmouth, in Norfolk, and claimed to have shot it down in flames.

On 20 August, *Luftflotte* 2 decreed that all Ju 88s sent on *Nachtjagd* patrols over England would carry bombs, and that all new aircraft delivered to II./NJG 1 had to be equipped with bomb racks with immediate effect. There would be one more success in August when Oberfeldwebel Merzbach of *Stab* II./NJG 1 claimed a Hurricane near Grimsby on the night of the 27th – another victory that cannot be substantiated. The next claim for the *Gruppe* was made by recently commissioned Oberleutnant Kurt Herrmann of 4./NJG 1 (presumably flying a Ju 88C-2) on the night of 8 September (an unidentified Blenheim downed near RAF Waddington, in Lincolnshire). The following night, Feldwebel Hermann Sommer of 5./NJG 1 used a Do 17Z-10 to claim another unidentified aircraft destroyed.

On 11 September II./NJG 1 became I./NJG 2, and five days later, the Ju 88C-2 flown by Feldwebel Werner Palm of 1. *Staffel* failed to return from a sortie over Britain.

At last, at 2130 hrs on 20 October, the first confirmed victory occurred when Hauptmann Karl Hülshoff of 3./NJG 2 claimed what he thought was a Hampden near RAF Dishforth, in North Yorkshire. It would appear that he had in fact downed a No 58 Sqn Whitley flown by Plt Off Ernest Brown, the aircraft crashing at Ingleby Barwick, also in North Yorkshire. Four crew, including the pilot, were killed and one severely injured.

Four nights later, Oberleutnant Kurt Herrmann claimed two Blenheims near RAF Hemswell, in Lincolnshire, one of which came from No 17

Operational Training Unit (OTU). However, both aircraft were only damaged. Feldwebel Hans Hahn of 3./NJG 2 also claimed his first victory of the war that night when he downed a Whitley of No 102 Sqn flown by Plt Off Anthony Davies. The latter had just retracted the aircraft's undercarriage after taking off from RAF Linton-on-Ouse, in North Yorkshire, on a mission to bomb Lünen, in Germany. The following report was later submitted by Davies;

'On attaining a height of 1,400 ft the pilot observed tracer to his left and below, and also immediately noticed tracer which he estimated was passing through the starboard wing tanks. At the time he was executing a left-hand circuit of the flare path. He throttled back, turned the navigation lights and petrol off, and observed a fire underneath the starboard main plane. Height was lost and an attempt was made to trim the aircraft with the elevator tabs but they did not function. He saw the ground vaguely through the light of the fire and opened the escape hatch. Fire was not intense.

'The aircraft struck a tree and flames immediately spread all over the cabin. He hit his head on the roof, but managed to scramble through the hatch and fell backwards to the ground, and then ran a few yards away. He then went back to the aircraft, and attempted to release Sgt Wilson, who was caught on a projection in the aircraft by his parachute harness. His hair was on fire but Plt Off Davies put the flames out with his hands. Plt Off Davies was unable to release Sgt Wilson but the latter was able to release himself after about 30 seconds. Plt Off Davies then saw the tail gunner, Plt Off Lee, fleeing from the tail. He called him and told him to run away from the aircraft and get down beside a nearby railway embankment.

'The fire was then much too intense to get near the aircraft. One or two bombs exploded, also a tank and some pyrotechnics. Plt Off Davies rallied the two survivors and ran to the railway line just as another bomb went off, and he ordered them to lie flat in a ditch. They eventually crossed the line and lay down beside the far embankment. Three or four bombs went off while they were there, and pyrotechnics fell all around them.'

Both Plt Off Terry Lee and Sgt Angus Wilson would succumb to their injuries on 2 November, and two more crew perished in the crash, leaving only Davies, who was injured, as the sole survivor.

Hahn, formerly of 9./KG 54, would claim a further 12 aircraft as an intruder pilot, being commissioned and awarded the Knight's Cross in July 1941, before becoming the final I./NJG 2 *Fernnachtjagd* combat loss on 12 October 1941.

October 1940 would also see the creation of 4./NJG 2, commanded by former 8./KG 54 pilot Oberleutnant Paul Bohn (the original *Staffelführer*, Oberleutnant Paul Zimmermann, had perished in a flying accident on 18 October prior to the unit converting to the Ju 88). Formed from elements of Bf 110-equipped I./ZG 2, 4. *Staffel* would remain under the control of I./NJG 2 until the end of February 1942, when it finally joined II./NJG 2.

On 1 November 1940, Unteroffizier Mathias Lang of 3./NJG 2 failed to return from an operational flight, his Ju 88C-4 being the first of its type to be lost. That night I./NJG 2 reported dropping five SC 50 bombs on RAF Feltwell, in Norfolk. The next claims by Ju 88 crews did not occur for more than three weeks.

In August 1940, II./NJG 1 was formed under Major Karl-Friedrich Heyse, an experienced bomber pilot who had previously commanded 2./KG 55. He would be reported missing over the North Sea on 23 November 1940, II./NJG 1 having by then been redesignated I./NJG 2 (*Author's collection*)

Luftwaffe records state that during *Fernnachtjagd* missions on the night of 23 November, Hauptmann Karl Hülshoff of 3./NJG 2 carried out three attacks on a Wellington that crashed into the sea 80 km west of Scheveningen, in the Netherlands. Ten minutes later, Feldwebel Heinz Strüning of 1./NJG 2 claimed a second Wellington 50 km west of Scheveningen. A third victory was credited to Oberleutnant Kurt Herrmann of 1./NJG 2, who claimed a Hampden destroyed northeast of The Wash, on the east coast of England. Only one aircraft was in fact lost over the North Sea that night – a Wellington of No 214 Sqn flown by Sgt Stanley Chester.

The intruders also reported dropping ten SC 50 bombs on RAF Catfoss, on the Yorkshire coast, and 20 SC 50s on Lincoln.

However, losses that night for I./NJG 2 were not good. The first casualty occurred when a 50 kg bomb exploded prematurely at Gilze-Rijen, destroying a Ju 88 and killing two groundcrew. Several hours later, Ju 88C-4s flown by *Gruppenkommandeur* Major Karl-Heinrich Heyse and Feldwebel Kurt Schlicht of 3./NJG 2 failed to return from missions over the North Sea. The possible demise of one of the intruders could be explained by the following report filed by Sgt Rupert Oakley, who was at the controls of a Hampden from No 61 Sqn that night;

'Sgt Oakley encountered three enemy aircraft when 90 miles off the English coast. They were identified as Ju 88s and were black in colour, with no visible markings. Sgt Oakley was forced down from 9,000ft to 2,000ft, at which point he jettisoned his bombs in order to add to his manoeuvrability. He and his crew had the satisfaction of dismissing one of the attackers, which was seen falling into the sea with its cockpit ablaze, and driving off the others.'

Heyse would be replaced by Hauptmann Karl Hülshoff and command of 3./NJG 2 went to Oberleutnant Ulrich Meyer, whose time as *Staffelkapitän* would last just 27 days.

The next victory was not recorded until 17 December, when Feldwebel Wilhelm Beier of 3./NJG 2 claimed a Hurricane over the sea east of Spilsby, in Lincolnshire. Three aircraft were active that morning, with the airfield at RAF Scampton, in Lincolnshire being attacked by two Ju 88Cs. Oberleutnant Paul Bohn of 4./NJG 2 claimed a Hampden over the airfield, while Beier, having shot down the Hurricane, headed to RAF Waddington and dropped his bombs. The identity of Beier's victim has not been determined.

Four days later, on 21 December, a more concerted series of dawn intruder missions occurred. I./NJG 2 reported attacking Selby, in North Yorkshire, Lincoln and Gainsborough, both in Lincolnshire, and Kings Lynn, in Norfolk. The RAF airfields of Hemswell, Scampton, West Raynham, in Norfolk, and Honington, in Suffolk, were also targeted, as were six ships in The Wash. Unteroffizier Gerhard Blum of 1./NJG 2 claimed a Blenheim off Kings Lynn which again cannot be identified.

In return, the aircraft flown by Oberleutnant Ulrich Meyer, recently appointed *Staffelkapitän* of 3./NJG 2, was listed as missing. According to an RAF report;

'This aircraft flew over RAF Manby [in Lincolnshire], at about 175 ft and was engaged by machine gun fire. It is understood that the aircraft was operating in company with others in the vicinity. There was evidence that the cabin had been set on fire and the pilot killed. The aircraft was blown to bits on impact.'

Meyer's Ju 88C-2 crashed near Louth, in Lincolnshire, killing all on board. Command of 3./NJG 2 now passed to Oberleutnant Paul Semrau, another former Z.St./KG 30 pilot. A second Ju 88C-2 flown by Gefreiter Kurt Ludescher of 1./NJG 2 crashed on landing at Gilze-Rijen, also killing all three crew

The intruders returned during the evening of 21 December, and a Do 17Z-10 crew from 2./NJG 2 claimed a Blenheim which yet again has never been identified. That was it as far as intruder claims and losses for 1940 were concerned, but 1941 would see an increase in such missions. Indeed they subsequently continued for a further nine months.

It would not be long before the first claims of the new year came. Just one intruder was active on 1 January 1941, the aircraft being flown by Leutnant Rudolf Stradner of 1./NJG 2. He visited York and Hull, in Yorkshire, and RAF Grantham, in Lincolnshire, before claiming a Wellington east of Lowestoft at 1840 hrs. Two such bombers were lost that night, both from No 301 Sqn. However, the aircraft flown by Sqn Ldr Stefan Floryanowicz crashed on land near RAF Digby, in Lincolnshire, at 2225 hrs, while the other Wellington, flown by Flg Off Boleslaw Murawski, crashed at Wellingore, south of Lincoln. Stradner's Ju 88 returned with combat damage. The bomber credited to Stradner would be his only victory prior to him being killed on operations on 9 July 1941.

The results for the next two nights were a little more positive for 3./NJG 2. On the 2nd, four intruders attacked RAF Scampton, and York and Ripon in North Yorkshire, with Unteroffizier Helmut Arnold of 1./NJG 2 claiming a Wellington 50 km east of the coastal village of Happisburgh, in Norfolk – no Wellingtons were lost. That same night, Feldwebel Hans Hahn of 3./NJG 2 downed his second Whitley from No 102 Sqn, the bomber being flown by Flg Off Desmond Coutts. Then, on 3 January, six intruders attacked Lincoln and Lowestoft, while Leutnant Gerhard Böhme of 3./NJG 2 claimed a Whitley 30 km east of Flamborough Head, on the Yorkshire coast. He appears to have engaged the aircraft flown by Plt Off Gerald Williams, who subsequently stated;

'On the way out at 1752hrs at 2,000ft, a multi-red Verey cartridge light was observed ahead, followed by a burst of tracer bullets, and this coincides with the position of an enemy aircraft reported near RAF Catterick [in North Yorkshire]. No damage or casualties were sustained.'

The time of the attack also coincides with Böhme's dubious claim.

Only two more incidents of note occurred in January (albeit a pilot from 2./NJG 2 possibly flying a Do 17Z-10 did make two claims in the early hours of the 16th). The Ju 88C-2 flown by Unteroffizier Otto Krähler of 3./NJG 2 failed to return from a mission on the night of the 9th, and on

Major Karl Hülshoff previously commanded 7./KG 54 prior to being made *Staffelkapitän* of 6./NJG 1, which then became 3./NJG 2. He would take over as *Gruppenkommandeur* of I./NJG 2 following the death of Major Heyse in November 1940 (*Author's collection*)

Oberleutnant Kurt Herrmann of 1./NJG 2 stands by his Ju 88C-4, its fin adorned with nine victory bars. Two of these were achieved over Poland in September 1939 whilst flying Bf 110s with 2.(*Zerstörer*)/LG 1, while the remaining seven were claimed during intruder missions over Britain in 1940–41. It would appear he was not flying this aircraft when he was forced to crash-land in England due to engine failure on 10 March 1941, as RAF intelligence reports detailing the wreckage of the Ju 88C-4 made no mention of such markings. Herrmann had been recommended for the Knight's Cross, but because he was captured before he could receive this award he was presented with the German Cross in Gold instead while held as a PoW in Canada (*Author's collection*)

29 January two Ju 88 crews from 1./NJG 2 apparently claimed seven barrage balloons destroyed over London.

February 1941 would be a more successful month. From a Ju 88C perspective, just one aircraft was lost returning from operations, but crews in turn claimed ten aircraft destroyed over England. The most successful night was the 10th, which also saw conventional German bombers attacking a number of airfields. In addition to two aircraft claimed by Hauptmann Rolf Jung and Oberleutnant Albert Schulz of 2./NJG 2, Oberleutnant Paul Semrau of 3./NJG 2 was credited with downing two Blenheims near RAF Feltwell. The bombers were probably from No 21 Sqn, which had the aircraft flown by Sqn Ldr John Sabine and Sgt Bert Chattaway shot down. Chattaway and one of his crew were killed, the remainder surviving.

The other successful pilot that night was Oberleutnant Kurt Herrmann of 1./NJG 2, who claimed two Hampdens over RAF Waddington. These were from Nos 49 and 144 Sqn, the former, flown by Sgt John Butterworth, being shot down (he and one other crewman were killed), and the latter, flown by Sgt Bill McVie, badly damaged.

On 15 February Feldwebel Heinz Strüning of 1./NJG 2 claimed a Hudson 75 km east of Great Yarmouth. At 0825 hrs (almost exactly the same time as was recorded in the German combat report), a Hudson of No 206 Sqn flown by Sqn Ldr Oliver Dias, which was on patrol off Great Yarmouth, encountered a Ju 88. The bomber's gunner got in a good burst of 250 rounds before the Ju 88 'dived into cloud streaming smoke'. It would appear that the gunner had indeed hit his target, for a Ju 88C-2 of I./NJG 2 later landed back at Gilze-Rijen with 20 per cent combat damage. No damage was inflicted on the Hudson in return, despite Strüning's claim.

That night, the *Fernnachtjäger* were back when, together with bombers, Ju 88s attacked a series of airfields. Claims by Strüning (a Wellington 65 km off Southend, in Essex) and Oberleutnant Herbert Bönsch of 1./NJG 2 were again optimistic, as two No 44 Sqn Hampdens reported being damaged, the crews landing safely, and an Oxford of No 2 Service Flying Training School (SFTS) force-landed at Fulbeck, in Lincolnshire. This aircraft was presumably the 'Blenheim' claimed by Bönsch over nearby RAF Waddington.

On 25 February Feldwebel Ernst Ziebarth of 1./NJG 2 shot down a Wellington of No 218 Sqn flown by Sgt Ron Hoos. Four crew were injured when the bomber force-landed near Swaffham, in Norfolk. The following night, in another series of attacks on bomber airfields in eastern England, the last two claims of the month were made by 1./NJG 2. Oberleutnant Bönsch's Blenheim near RAF Scampton cannot be confirmed, while Oberleutnant Kurt Herrmann's 'Blenheim' near RAF Waddington was in fact another Oxford, this time from No 2 Central Flying School (CFS), based at RAF Cranwell, in Lincolnshire. The Oxford crashed at Fulbeck, killing Flt Lt Desmond Trench. This would be Herrmann's ninth, and final, claim, for 11 days later he was taken prisoner.

March started quietly for I./NJG 2. On the first night of the month, its aircraft attacked Boston, in Lincolnshire, Hull, Norwich and RAF Bircham Newton, both in Norfolk, Lincoln and RAF Scampton, with Oberleutnant Herbert Bönsch claiming to have intercepted a Blenheim over the latter site and striking it in the fuselage, after which it caught fire. No RAF losses match this claim, however. Over Norwich, a Ju 88C-4 was hit by anti-aircraft and lost an engine, resulting in it crash-landing back at Gilze-Rijen.

Very little occurred for the next eight days until 2350 hrs on 10 March when a Ju 88C-4 of 1./NJG 2 slid to a halt at Terrington St Clement, in Norfolk. Oberleutnant Kurt Herrmann had suffered double engine failure caused by the connecting rod on the starboard engine shearing and going through the crank case and the port engine overheating due to failure of the oil system. All three crew were captured, but only the Bordfunker was injured when the aircraft tipped onto its starboard wing, trapping him. The crew was prevented from setting fire to their aircraft because of this. The RAF finally had a relatively undamaged example of a Ju 88C, allowing it to ascertain exactly what it was up against. An intelligence report on the aircraft noted;

'Armament: one MG 151 belt fed below three MG 17s, all fixed and firing forward out of a nose, which was covered. These guns were fitted around the bomb aimer's position and were fired by one press button on the pilot's control column. Armoured bulkhead 11mm thick was fitted in the nose immediately in front of the ammunition containers and in front of the pilot's seat, which is slotted to allow the guns to pass through. Bulletproof glass was also fitted in front of the gunsight. One MG 17 in lower gunner's position with no armour protection.

Ju 88C-2/C-4 of I./NJG 2 clearly showing the *Nachtjagdgeschwader*'s *Englandblitz* insignia. This aircraft lacks flame dampeners but it is fitted with a 20 mm MG FF cannon in the nose, along with three 7.92 mm MG 17 machine guns. Note the all-black camouflage adopted by I./NJG 2's intruders (*Author's collection*)

'All the forward guns were belt fed on a lengthy and complicated belting system. The feed for the MG 17s was taken from two containers fitted between the pilot's legs, with the rudder pedals either side, and one container on the aft starboard side of the cabin. No external bomb racks were fitted but internal racks were provided for eight 50kg bombs in the rear bomb compartment.'

Although nine more Ju 88C-4s from I./NJG 2 would crash on mainland England over the next seven months, none revealed as much as this aircraft did. Herrmann was the top scoring *Fernnachtjagd* pilot at the time of his capture with a total of nine victories, and he confirmed to his captors that he had flown 59 war flights, of which 25 were over England, 14 over Poland and 20 over Norway. Being I./NJG 2's leading ace, Herrmann had been recommended for a Knight's Cross the previous month, but his capture put paid to this. He would have to wait until October 1942 to eventually receive the German Cross in Gold whilst held in captivity.

The remainder of March 1941 would see Feldwebel Hans Hahn of 3./NJG 2 take his score to four, with a Blenheim downed in the early hours of the 13th (possibly from No 21 Sqn, whose Sqn Ldr Arthur Allen reported encountering fighters on his return flight, with his gunner being wounded) and a Manchester that same evening (from No 207 Sqn, flown by Flg Off Hugh Matthews).

The final two claims for 1./NJG 2 came at dawn on 18 March. Feldwebel Peter Laufs was credited with a Wellington for his seventh victory (a No 221 Sqn aircraft reported being attacked by what the crew took to be a Bf 110 off the coast, the nightfighter causing very minor damage). Shortly thereafter, Leutnant Rudolf Pfeiffer also downed a Wellington, with the No 149 Sqn aircraft flown by Sgt Ron Warren being shot down while trying to land at RAF Mildenhall, in Suffolk.

Of greater concern to I./NJG 2 was the loss of 4. *Staffel's* Ju 88C-4 flown by Gefreiter Hans Körner on 14 March, this aircraft being the unit's first of the year to be confirmed shot down by a nightfighter. A Beaufighter of No 29 Sqn flown by Wg Cdr Charles Widdows had closed in unseen by the Ju 88 crew and fired one burst that entered the fuselage, after which the aircraft went into a dive, caught fire and broke up in the air, spreading itself over an area of two miles and, unsurprisingly, killing its crew. The smashed remains revealed very little, especially as the RAF had acquired an almost complete example of a Ju 88C-4 just four days earlier.

4./NJG 2 would lose a second aircraft on the night of 30 March. Three Ju 88Cs were active, with crews reporting attacking RAF Driffield, in the East Riding of Yorkshire, and a Blenheim near RAF Finningley, in South Yorkshire. Despite the aircraft being attacked three times, no claim was made. At some stage during the night, Gefreiter Otto Krüger's Ju 88C-4 disappeared, and it is assumed the aircraft crashed in the North Sea due to engine failure. The only RAF aircraft reporting intruders was a Wellington from No 150 Sqn flown by Sgt Victor Coleman, which suffered a punctured starboard wheel and fuel tank following an attack.

For I./NJG 2, April 1941 would prove to be the most successful month to date, with 25 claims over England. Leutnant Heinz Völker of 3. *Staffel* led the way with five victories, taking his score to seven overall. Three of his successes that month came on the night of the 24th when he claimed three Blenheims at RAF Lindholme, in South Yorkshire, with his Bordfunker Feldwebel Herbert Biehne getting another (his other crew member was Bordmechaniker Feldwebel Hermann Gärtner). Völker's crew provided the following report;

'During a night fighter mission over East England, one of the aircraft (crew – Lt Völker, Fw Biehne and Fw Gärtner) shot down four enemy Bristol Blenheim aircraft over Lindholme airfield.

'0030hrs, one Bristol Blenheim was attacked at 300m altitude, the aeroplane crashed burning. On impact a very heavy explosion was observed.

'0037hrs, the second kill followed at 100m altitude. After firing, the enemy aircraft lost single parts and flick-rolled to the left.

'0044hrs, the third enemy aircraft was attacked at 150m altitude, tipped over the left wing and crashed on fire.

'0050hrs, the Bordfunker, Fw Biehne, shot down the fourth opponent at 150m altitude. The enemy aircraft crashed vertically, the crew watching the burning aeroplane on the ground when flying over it.

'Then, at 0100hrs, five SC 50 and five SD 50 [bombs] were dropped on Lindholme airfield without observed effect.'

Three Blenheims from No 54 OTU were indeed attacked that night, with two aircraft – one flown by future ace Sgt Arthur Spurgin and the other by Sgt George Attenborough – damaged and former Battle of Britain pilot Flt Lt Richard Denison forced to bail out of the third machine. This success was reported in Berlin, but strangely it did not result in any major award for Völker and his crew.

Feldwebel Hans Hahn of 1./NJG 1 took his tally to eight during the course of the month, while Oberfeldwebel Hermann Sommer (with his crew of Feldwebel Otto Glas and Oberfeldwebel Heinz Reinagel) of 2./NJG 2 (this *Staffel* now appearing to be in the process of converting from the Do 17Z-10 to the Ju 88C-4) claimed three Blenheims and a Beaufort on 30 April. Sommer's successes came near RAF airfields in the Tollerton, Hucknall (both in Nottinghamshire) and Bircham Newton areas, taking his score to five.

This Ju 88C-4 of I./NJG 2 featured victory bars on its rudder, although who achieved these kills remains unidentified. All unit and aircraft markings have been blackened, including the spinners that would normally have exhibited *Staffel* colours of white, red or yellow for 1., 2. and 3./NJG 2, respectively (*Author's collection*)

Strangely, the only casualty than can be matched to these claims is a No 2 CFS Oxford at RAF Tollerton. It has also been suggested that Sommer was responsible for shooting down a Wellington flown by Sgt Frank Hewitson of No 99 Sqn, but the final radio transmission from this aircraft, made almost three hours after Sommer's last claim, stated that the crew was homing in on another airfield.

I./NJG 2 lost three aircraft this month, two of which came from 4. *Staffel*. The first of these fell on 9 April when Gefreiter Franz Brotz's Ju 88C was downed by Sgt Stanley Bennett in a No 25 Sqn Beaufighter, the aircraft crashing near Oakham in Rutland. Brotz was killed and his aircraft totally destroyed, but the two remaining crew were captured and their interrogation revealed more on the *Gruppe*. For example, the Bordfunker had flown previously with Oberfeldwebel Martin Jeschke, formerly of the *Legion Condor* and Z.St./KG 30, and had seen combat in Poland and Norway during the course of 63 operational flights. He also stated that I./NJG 2 had so far shot down 38 aircraft.

The *Staffel's* second loss, on 17 April, is a bit of a mystery. At 2123 hrs, an aircraft dived into the ground vertically and on fire near Thorney, in Cambridgeshire. In 1978, the wreckage was excavated, whereupon it was discovered that this was a Ju 88C-4 flown by Obergefreiter Wilhelm Beetz. His remains, together with those of the two members of his crew, were discovered and subsequently buried at the German Military Cemetery at Cannock Chase, in Staffordshire. No bombs were found nor was there any evidence of bullet or cannon strikes. It has also been suggested that this aircraft was shot down by another intruder, but no claims were submitted that night by either the Luftwaffe or the RAF.

The final aircraft lost that month was a 3. *Staffel* machine, which crashed at Dongen, north of Gilze-Rijen, on 18 April, killing its crew.

An improvement in the weather and an increase in the intensity of RAF Bomber Command's attacks allowed I./NJG 2 to claim 13 victories during May 1941. As it transpired, however, four of these aircraft had merely been damaged and five cannot be linked to any RAF losses. On a more positive note, no Ju 88s had been lost in combat that month. Again, recently promoted Oberfeldwebel Hans Hahn was particularly successful, claiming what he thought was a Fulmar near RAF Coltishall, in Norfolk, on 4 May and a Blenheim the following night. The Fulmar was in fact a Spitfire of No 222 Sqn flown by Plt Off Bernard Klee. The unit's unofficial diary noted;

'That night seven 50kg bombs were dropped in a field in front of the Officers' Mess by a Ju 88; no damage resulted. Later, two Spitfires flown by Plt Off Klee and Sgt Burgess took off to patrol base. Soon the Controller warned both pilots who were patrolling independently that an e/a [enemy aircraft] was orbiting with them, and we on the ground could plainly see the e/a manoeuvring to get on their tails. The Junkers was continually weaving, making steep turns and otherwise evading our aircraft.

'Sgt Burgess managed to get e/a in his sights and was about to open fire when e/a fired two star cartridges (two reds), which dazzled him and caused him to loose e/a. He next saw two bursts of tracer flash past his aircraft without doing any damage. At 0330hrs observers on the ground saw a Spitfire (now known to be Plt Off Klee) fly straight across the aerodrome from north to south followed by e/a, who fired a burst of cannon shells at the Spitfire which crashed in flames to the south-east of the aerodrome and was burnt out.'

Plt Off Klee was killed, and the diary entry concluded by saying;

'The exhausts from the Spitfires showed up very plainly, whereas the e/a's exhaust was not visible. The speed and manoeuvrability of the e/a was truly remarkable.'

That night, I./NJG 2 reported attacking RAF airfields at Feltwell, Watton (Norfolk), Bridlington, Leconfield (both East Riding of Yorkshire) and Grantham. The 40-minute engagement by Hahn and his crew of Unteroffiziere Ernst-Wilhelm Meissler and Helmut Scheidt with the Fulmar (Klee's Spitfire) was also noted.

No Blenheims were recorded as being attacked on the night of 5 May, but a Hurricane flown by Battle of Britain veteran Sgt Reg Parrott of RAF Coltishall-based No 257 Sqn was shot down while attempting to land at RAF Duxford, in Cambridgeshire. The unit's unofficial diary noted;

'Sgt Parrott took off on a night weather test at midnight and was ordered to land at Duxford as an enemy aircraft was in the vicinity of RAF Coltishall. He proceeded to Duxford, put on his navigation lights and, whilst circling preparatory to landing, was shot down in flames four miles north east of the aerodrome by an unidentified and unplotted enemy aircraft. He was killed instantly. Coltishall was bombed by the e/a which prevented Parrott from landing.'

The same diarist that recorded Parrott's demise also noted for 5 May;

'Just after midnight, raider dropped a stick of bombs between the Officers' Mess and No 5 Barrack Block. One airman was killed and five others injured. They were standing in and about the doorway of the Block where some windows were blown in; otherwise no damage.'

Again, I./NJG 2 had been very active that night, attacking Great Yarmouth, RAF Digby, Lincoln, RAF Waddington, Newmarket, in Suffolk, and RAF Leconfield. Hahn's claim for a Blenheim at RAF Feltwell, northeast of Duxford, came at 0113 hrs, while Parrott is reported to have crashed just two minutes later. The Luftwaffe recorded that this was Hahn's tenth victory over eastern England, and it was followed by promotion to Leutnant and the award of the Knight's Cross on 9 July. His success in aerial combat and the sinking of a freighter off Dunkirk in May 1940 when still with 9./KG 54 were seen as justification for the decoration. Hahn's next victory would not come until 16 August, and just under two months later he and his regular crew of Meissler and Scheidt, neither of whom received any major award, would be dead.

June 1941 would see a further 21 claims made by I./NJG 2, of which four resulted in aircraft being damaged, not destroyed, and 11 cannot be positively linked to any RAF losses. One of those damaged, on the night of the 17th, was a Wellington of No 142 Sqn flown by Flt Lt Alexander Gosman who subsequently recalled;

'We were about an hour out on our way to Duisburg when Sgt Doug Maclean told me there was somebody following us. We were fairly high, approaching our operational height, and at that time of year it is fairly light. I turned south towards the dark and our follower turned with us and opened fire.

'Simultaneously, fire also came at us from ahead – i.e. from the south. There was no sound from the rear turret and something told me instinctively that Maclean was dead. Durham, the navigator, jettisoned our load as we headed down, fast, and turned for home with the undercarriage hanging loose and all hydraulics gone. We could see one of our attackers following us, but as we were almost at wave-top height, he apparently gave up and disappeared. We managed the rest of the journey fairly easily and belly flopped in the dark on the edge of the airfield at [RAF] Binbrook [in Lincolnshire] away from the flare path.'

No other Wellingtons were lost that night. Gosman's attacker was almost certainly Oberleutnant Herbert Bönsch, who claimed his sixth aircraft – a Wellington – at 0008 hrs 115 km east of Cromer, on the Norfolk coast. He scored his seventh victory six nights later.

It is interesting to note that this month finally saw the RAF formally acknowledge that these intruder operations were indeed taking place. With an effective nightfighter force still in the process of evolving, the RAF published tactics on what to do if enemy intruders were reported in the vicinity. Essentially, RAF bomber crews were told to divert immediately to an airfield further north and west, where intruders had not been reported. However, for some, diverting at the end of a raid in a damaged aircraft with dead and wounded crew onboard was not always that easy.

In addition to Oberleutnant Herbert Bönsch, the other successful pilots in June 1941 were Oberfeldwebel Hermann Sommer of 2. *Staffel*, who took his score to nine on the 27th, Oberfeldwebel Wilhelm Beier of 3. *Staffel*, who claimed his sixth on the 13th, and Oberleutnant Paul Semrau, also from 3./NJG 2, who took his tally to five, again on 13 June. Only Semrau's victory, a Halifax over RAF Finningley, can be positively linked to a loss – a Wellington of No 25 OTU flown by Sgt Walter Collyer, which was shot down in the circuit, killing the crew.

These successes came at a high price, with I./NJG 2 suffering its greatest number of losses to date. First to be killed was Leutnant Josef Feuerbaum (and his crew) from 2. *Staffel*. No doubt hoping to increase his score of three victories so far, he flew his Ju 88 into a hillside near Whitby, in North Yorkshire, in poor visibility just after midnight on 4 June. Eight unexploded 50 kg bombs were found in the wreckage, proof that Feuerbaum had not yet begun attacking airfields that night.

The next two aircraft to be lost fell on the night of 13–14 June, and both came from 4./NJG 2. The first, flown by Unteroffizier Richard Hoffmann, was shot down by Sqn Ldr Harold 'Flash' Pleasance of Beaufighter-equipped No 25 Sqn. The crew bailed out after the first attack and the aircraft crashed near Swaffham, five of the bombs still being carried by the Ju 88C-4 exploding on impact. Hoffmann and one of his crew survived, but they could reveal little to their interrogators as they had only joined 4. *Staffel* in April 1941 and this was just their fourth flight.

Oberfeldwebel Wilhelm Beier of 3./NJG 2 poses alongside 14 victory bars marked onto the tail of his Ju 88C-4. His first success came on 17 December 1940 and his 14th on 8 August 1941, and this run of success would result in him receiving the Knight's Cross on 10 October 1941. Beier survived the war with a total of 38 victories to his name (*Author's collection/ Thomas Knauf*)

No 25 Sqn also claimed the second of the *Staffel*'s aircraft lost that night when Plt Off David Thompson sent Unteroffizier Helmut Bähner's machine crashing into marshes near Kings Lynn. Although the crew were killed and the aircraft destroyed, eight 50 kg bombs were discovered, proving that they too had only just arrived over England. Of interest, one victory stripe was noted on the tail with the date 9 April 1941. This was probably Unteroffizier Hans Berschwinger's aircraft that night, for he downed a Wellington of No 211 Sqn (flown by Plt Off Peter Brown) shortly after it had taken off from RAF Bircham Newton's satellite field. A report by the unit on the incident noted;

'Aircraft R1049 on local night flying programme at Langham satellite aerodrome was intercepted by an enemy aircraft believed to be a Ju 88. Both aircraft opened fire simultaneously. Our aircraft was set on fire in the air and crashed out of control at Burnham Westgate. The crew were all killed, this being the Squadron's first casualty.'

Berschwinger, who would later be awarded the Honour Goblet of the Luftwaffe and the German Cross in Gold (the latter posthumously), would eventually be killed on 16 February 1944 while still with 4./NJG 2, having by then shot down 11 aircraft.

To make matters worse for 4. *Staffel* on the night of 13–14 June, Unteroffizier Vitus Alt clipped the water with the wingtip of his Ju 88C-2 while circling a dinghy that contained survivors from a ditched He 111 from 8./KG 4. The aircraft cartwheeled into the North Sea, killing the crew.

Losses did not end there this month for I./NJG 2. At 0120 hrs on 22 June the Ju 88C-4 flown by Oberfeldwebel Otto Wiese was intercepted by Flg Off Michael Herrick of No 25 Sqn during a mission in what was termed the Raum (patrol) B area. The only survivor, Bordfunker Unteroffizier Heinrich Beul, recorded what happened next;

'Our aircraft was hit from behind. Our starboard wing, with two 400-litre fuel tanks in it, caught fire. Otto went into a steep dive in an attempt to extinguish the flames but to no avail – in fact the flames got bigger. Otto gave the order to bail out and Gefreiter Hermann Mandel tried to open the bottom gondola but couldn't, its handle having been damaged by a cannon shell. We had to jettison the cockpit hood. I stepped onto my seat and rolled out. I was lucky to get out first and immediately tried to pull my parachute release. I was spinning over and over. I reached the handle and pulled. There was a tremendous jerk and I swung like a pendulum.'

The fighter crashed at a shallow angle at Deeping St James, in Lincolnshire. Again, the crew had not dropped their eight 50 kg bombs, as five were found in the wreckage.

There would be one more 4. *Staffel* casualty in June 1941. Just after midnight on the 26th, *Staffelkapitän* Oberleutnant Paul Bohn was closing in on his fifth victim when he was killed by return fire. Bordmechaniker Unteroffizier Walter Lindner pulled the pilot's body out of its seat and turned the fighter for home. When over mainland France, he attached a static line to Bohn's parachute and pushed him out, before he and Bordfunker Feldwebel Hans Engmann also bailed out. They landed near Charleville, while Bohn's body was found 12 days later at Eclaibes, south of Maubeuge on the France–Belgium border. As to the Ju 88, it continued southwards, and when the aircraft's ample fuel reserves ran out, the fighter crashed near Milan, in Italy.

Just prior to being killed, Bohn was credited with downing a Whitley at 0015 hrs, although none were lost that night. Oberfeldwebel Hermann Jung, also of 4./NJG 2, claimed a Whitley in the same location 20 minutes later. The only unaccounted RAF loss on 25–26 June was a Wellington flown by Sgt John Hancock of No 99 Sqn, which is believed to have crashed into the North Sea. Flg Off William Villers of No 49 Sqn reported an encounter with a nightfighter, and he only missed being rammed by pushing his Hampden's nose down and allowing the German aircraft to pass overhead. Sgt Peter Griffin, flying a Whitley of No 51 Sqn, reported being attacked by what he took to be a Bf 110 75 miles northwest of the Dutch island of Texel, his bomber suffering slight damage. He jettisoned his bombs and landed safely at 0210 hrs. This was Griffin's first operational flight, and he was destined to be shot down and killed by ace Oberleutnant Helmut Lent of 4./NJG 1 on 15 August 1941.

Following Bohn's loss, command of 4. *Staffel* passed to Oberleutnant Hans-Georg Schütze, formerly of 2. *Staffel*.

Of note, the *Gruppe*'s 100th victory went to Oberfeldwebel Hermann Sommer (his ninth) of 2./NJG 2 on 27 June, although the identity of the aircraft he claimed to have shot down remains unknown.

The first claims for July 1941 went to Oberfeldwebel Peter Laufs of 1./NJG 1 for a Battle near Wells-next-the-Sea, in Norfolk, at 0100 hrs on the 5th. According to the diary of Spitfire-equipped No 452 Sqn, at '0108hrs, Sgt A G Costello killed at Fen Lane Farm near North Somercotes after being attacked preparing to land at aerodrome. His Spitfire was completely destroyed.' Costello was Laufs' ninth victory of the war.

Between 5–30 July, I./NJG 2 would claim 19 aircraft, of which two were only damaged and eight unidentified. In addition to Oberfeldwebel Laufs,

Hauptmann Paul Semrau (left) was another pilot who flew with Z.St/KG 30 before becoming an intruder pilot with I./NJG 2 in 1940. Taking command of 3./NJG 2 following the death of Oberleutnant Ulrich Meyer on 21 December 1940, he received the Knight's Cross in October 1942 after claiming 14 victories. Eventually taking his tally to 46 kills, Semrau was awarded the Oak Leaves posthumously on 17 April 1945 after being killed in action two months previously, on 8 February, while serving as *Kommodore* of NJG 2 (*Author's collection*)

top scorers this month were recently promoted Oberfeldwebel Wilhelm Beier of 3./NJG 2, who took his score to 11 on 18 July, and Oberleutnant Paul Semrau, who took his score to eight that same night.

Another pilot with eight victories was Leutnant Heinz Völker of 3./NJG 2. His ninth success came at 0130 hrs on 22 July when he collided with a Wellington of No 11 OTU flown by Flt Sgt Walter Hannah and Sgt Bruce Thompson as it was preparing to land at RAF Bassingbourne, in Cambridgeshire. Both aircraft then crashed at Ashwell, in Hertfordshire, with the deaths of three German and eight RAF aircrew. The wreckage revealed very little apart from the fact Völker had not dropped his bombs, for they were found in the burnt-out remains.

Again, in addition to Völker and his crew, the *Gruppe* would suffer further losses. Leutnant Rudolf Stradner of 1./NJG 2 crashed off the Dutch coast on 9 July after having declared an emergency. There were no survivors. Then, on the 24th, the Ju 88C-4 of 4. *Staffel's* Obergefreiter Heinz Ladiges crashed at Bondy, in Lincolnshire. Twenty minutes after dropping his 50 kg bombs on RAF Elsham Wolds, also in Lincolnshire, his aircraft was seen to burst into flames, dive into the ground and explode, creating a crater 40 ft in diameter and scattering wreckage over a wide area. With no RAF nightfighter or Luftwaffe intruder crews making claims that night, Ladiges' aircraft was almost certainly brought down by light and/or heavy anti-aircraft fire.

The final loss for the month was Leutnant Dr Lothar Bisang of 2./NJG 2. At 0420 hrs on the 28th, his Ju 88C-4 dived vertically into the ground at Wivenhoe, in Essex. Bisang had just shot down his first aircraft – an Oxford of No 2 SFTS which was flying circuits at the Akeman Street landing ground northeast of Minster Lovell, in Oxfordshire, killing LAC Ralph Smith. Bisang's Bordfunker reported the success, but after that nothing. It has been suggested that Bisang panicked and lost control of his aircraft while manoeuvring to avoid interception by an RAF nightfighter he had spotted. Indeed, Plt Off Fred Burnard and Sgt Reeves of Havoc-equipped No 85 Sqn reported 'seeing an e/a crashing near Colchester [in Essex] for no particular reason that could be observed'.

Of possible concern to the RAF, the location of Bisang's claim was the furthest west of the intruder campaign to date. Until then, I./NJG 2 had operated in three Raum areas. Raum A covered East Anglia, Raum B Lincolnshire and Yorkshire and Raum C up to the Scottish borders.

It had been noted by the RAF that in the wreckage of Obergefreiter Heinz Ladige's aircraft, examined four days prior to the loss of Bisang's Ju 88C-4, fragments of a map had been found showing a patrol area which included Leicester, Woburn, Reading, Salisbury, Trowbridge and Gloucester – towns and cities near to where many training units, such as No 2 SFTS at RAF Brize Norton, in Oxfordshire, were located. It is believed this area was designated Raum F. Strangely, Bisang reported his success in Raum C, which was nowhere near the crash sites of the Oxford and his Ju 88. The identification of a new Raum would make little difference to the intruder campaign, which would soon come to an end.

The final two full months of *Fernnachtjagd* operations by I./NJG 2 saw 14 claims in August and four in September 1941. Again, a number of these cannot be matched, especially the three credited to Oberfeldwebel

Wilhelm Beier of 3. *Staffel* on 8 August which took his score to 14, and resulted in him receiving the Knight's Cross in October 1941. The other *Experten* in the *Gruppe* also made claims, with Oberfedlwebel Peter Laufs of 1. *Staffel* taking his score to ten, Leutnant Hans Hahn of 3. *Staffel* to 11, Oberfeldwebel Heinz Strüning, also of 1. *Staffel*, to eight and Oberleutnant Paul Semrau and Feldwebel Alfons Köster, both from 3. *Staffel*, to nine and ten, respectively.

Losses in combat totalled three aircraft, with Leutnant Rudolf Pfeiffer and Feldwebel Walter Kleine, both from 4./NJG 2, failing to return on 17 August and 2 September, respectively. In Kleine's crew was Feldwebel Hans Engmann, who had survived when Oberleutnant Paul Bohn was killed on 26 June. This time he was not so lucky, and his was the only body from Kleine's crew to be washed ashore in the Netherlands.

15 September saw the last Ju 88C intruder shot down over England. Its pilot, Oberfeldwebel Erwin Viel of 1./NJG 2, had only joined the *Staffel* at the end of June 1941, having flown operationally with 4./KG 51 in the battles of France and Britain, during the Blitz, over Yugoslavia and, finally, in the first week of the attack on the USSR. He claimed to have completed more than 60 missions as a bomber pilot and then 20 as an intruder before his luck ran out.

Coming in over the English coast at Southwold, in Suffolk, and having seen no RAF aircraft, Viel made for what he believed was RAF Stradishall, also in Suffolk. There, he dropped 50 kg bombs and then flew in the direction of Clacton-on-Sea, in Essex, before heading home. Once off the coast, the Ju 88C was intercepted by former bomber pilot Sqn Ldr Gordon Raphael, flying a Havoc from No 85 Sqn. After a 15-minute chase, and despite Viel's efforts to throw off his pursuer, a short burst hit the German fighter in the starboard wing, which then caught fire. The crew immediately bailed out and the Ju 88 crashed into the sea at 2125 hrs. Two crewmen swam to shore in Essex and the third was rescued by boat.

There was one more operational loss for the *Gruppe* during this period which could have had a far greater impact on I./NJG 2 than it did. On 12 August, 54 Blenheim IVs carried out a daring daylight attack on the power stations at Knapsack and Quadrath, near Köln. There was a massive RAF fighter presence during the operation, both to protect the bombers and divert German fighters. The Luftwaffe's response resulted in the destruction of 12 Blenheims (with more returning damaged) and six Spitfires.

That day, I./NJG 2 had been ordered to carry out patrols along the Dutch coastline. Feldwebel Vincenz Giessübel of 2./NJG 2 reported taking off on such a mission at 1302 hrs and landing again without incident at 1447 hrs, while Oberleutnant Heinz-Horst Hissbach of 1. *Staffel* carried out a similar task, with nothing to report. Another pilot involved was the *Gruppenkommandeur* of I./NJG 2, Hauptmann Karl Hülshoff, but his flight would be far from uneventful.

According to Battle of Britain ace Sqn Ldr Harborne Stephen, who was leading Spitfire-equipped No 234 Sqn on an offensive sweep and cover to the Blenheims on their way home;

'We were approaching the coast near Veere [in the Netherlands] when a twin-engined aircraft I had been watching decided to come and visit us. On approaching, he fired two series of four star cartridges in all. The cartridges broke up into four red stars after firing. I had identified him as an e/a some time back and was waiting until I had reassembled my squadron. At this point an Me 109 made a beam attack, developing into a quarter astern attack, on me, but this I evaded, gave him a quick burst, and did not worry more about him.

'As I resumed my course, the Ju 88 nightfighter, who was painted entirely black, gave me a quick burst with his front guns, but as he was on the beam, it was not accurate. I turned onto the tail of the Ju 88 and opened fire from about 150yds and immediately observed hits on the port wing, engine and fuselage. The fuselage finally began to tear open, but I transferred my fire to the port engine and gave it a three-second burst. The pilot then took immediate evasive action by shutting both throttles, causing me to close my range too fast while I was concentrating on my firing, and making me break away to starboard. I had the satisfaction of knowing that before I broke to starboard, the port engine of this aircraft was well alight and the e/a dived into cloud. I saw him once more but could not close the range, although we were at 1500ft.'

With a badly damaged Ju 88C-4, Hülshoff force landed at Steenbergen, due east of Veere, en route to Gilze-Rijen. Although he was unscathed, both Bordfunker Oberfeldwebel Willi Mayer and Bordschütze Oberfeldwebel Paul Licht were wounded.

October 1941 would be the last month of intruding over England for I./NJG 2, for on the 12th, the *Gruppe* was informed that it would be moving to Sicily to conduct operations over the Mediterranean. The reason for stopping intruder missions was simple – the *Führer* wanted to see RAF bombers burning on the ground in the Fatherland, where the German public could see them, rather than in England, where they could not.

As a result, there would be just three claims made that month, and one very serious loss. The first claim, on 3 October, was for a Stirling of No 7 Sqn flown by Sqn Ldr Don McLeod. While on approach to land at RAF Oakington, in Cambridgeshire, the bomber was attacked by Feldwebel Alfons Köster of 3./NJG 2. A ten-minute dogfight ensued, with the Ju 88 making six attacks at a height of 50 m. A second Stirling, flown by Sgt Sidney Matkin, attempted to come to McLeod's aid, but to no avail. On fire, two crew successfully bailed out before the bomber crashed at nearby Caxton Gibbet, killing the pilot and five crew. This was Köster's 11th victory.

A second victory came during the early hours of 11 October, when Oberfeldwebel Heinz Strüning of 1./NJG 2 claimed his ninth victory in the form of a Blenheim of No 51 OTU. It crashed at Sherrington, northeast of Milton Keynes, in Buckinghamshire, killing the aircraft's sole occupant, Sgt Francis Filmer.

I./NJG 2's final victory in this theatre would be a pyrrhic one. At 2130 hrs on the 12th, a Ju 88C-4 collided with an Oxford of No 12 SFTS over RAF Grantham. Both aircraft crashed, killing Sgt Tom Graham and Cpl Sam Edwards in the Oxford and the three unidentified German crewmen. Identification of the latter was made harder by the explosion of two bombs shortly after the aircraft crashed, although a collar patch of a Leutnant and a crew list for 3./NJG 2 were found in the wreckage. Also, 13 dated victories, starting on 17 December 1940 and ending with three on

Hans Hahn was formerly a bomber pilot before transferring to 3./NJG 2. Whilst with the unit he would claim 12 aircraft on intruder missions, receive a commission and be awarded the Knight's Cross. His run of aerial success came to an end near Grantham on 11 October 1941, when he was killed in a collision with his final victim (*Author's collection*)

8 August 1941, were found on a section of wreckage. These matched the claims made by Oberfeldwebel Hermann Beier of 3./NJG 2, who was credited with victories 12–14 on 8 August 1941. However, Beier, who had received the Knight's Cross on 10 October, was still very much alive. Indeed, he would survive the war.

That night, I./NJG 2 was active dropping bombs on RAF airfields at Honington, Cranwell, Driffield and Feltwell, plus two unidentified airfields and targets in Southwold and Ipswich, both in Suffolk. Although no aerial victory claims were made by either the RAF or the Luftwaffe on 12–13 October, I./NJG 2 reported that Leutnant Hans Hahn and his crew from 3. *Staffel* were missing.

Since being commissioned and receiving the Knight's Cross, Hahn had enjoyed little in the way of luck. He and Unteroffizier Helmut Scheidt were injured in a take-off accident on 31 July, and then suffered another accident on landing on 4 September. In between these dates, on 17 August, he had taken his score to 11 when he shot down a Wellington of No 104 Sqn near Scunthorpe, in Lincolnshire, killing Sgt Bill Stephenson and his crew.

Hahn's collision with the Oxford over Grantham took his final tally to 12. He and his two crewmen, Bordfunker Unteroffizier Ernst-Wilhelm Meissler and Bordmechaniker Unteroffizier Helmut Scheidt, were initially buried at Grantham but now lie at Cannock Chase.

It would appear that 11–12 October – the penultimate night of operations – saw a final flurry of attacks on RAF airfields, including Newmarket, Newton, Church Fenton, Kirton-in-Lindsey and Leconfield. Some 13 separate attacks were recorded, not to mention the shooting down of the No 51 OTU Blenheim – its demise was incorrectly recorded by the Luftwaffe as having taken place the following night.

Then, on the night of 13–14 October, just two intruders were active, dropping bombs on what was believed to be the RAF airfields at Feltwell, Hemswell and Manby, and Norwich. By then, 2./NJG 2, which continued to use a small number of Do 17Z-10s until the end of the year, was exclusively flying the Ju 88C-4 on operations. I./NJG 2's time over England had come to an end, and the intruders, in the form of Me 410s of V./KG 2, did not return in force until August 1943.

CHAPTER THREE

MEDITERRANEAN OPERATIONS

I./NJG 2 (which still included 4. *Staffel*) began leaving Gilze-Rijen, bound for Catania, on Sicily, on 9 November 1941. Twelve days later, 2. *Staffel's* Oberleutnant Heinz Harmstorf led six aircraft to Berka, near Benghazi in Libya, in response to the British offensive Operation *Crusader*. However, after the airfield had been bombed and the Ju 88Cs of Harmstorf and Leutnant Dieter Voigt damaged by anti-aircraft fire on 23 November, the aircraft returned to Catania on the 28th.

The first claim by I./NJG 2 in its new theatre of operations would not come until 12 December, when Leutnant Herbert Haas of 1. *Staffel* was credited with downing a Beaufighter south of Malta – this victory cannot be matched with any losses. However, the following day, Oberfeldwebel Hermann Sommer of 2./NJG 2 did indeed down a Beaufighter of No 272 Sqn south of Crete, killing Flg Off Graham Morris and Flt Sgt Henry Hilton. These successes proved that I./NJG 2 was undertaking daylight convoy escorts in addition to nightfighter missions and intruding over Malta.

By the end of December, claims had been made by Leutnante Peter Laufs (Beaufighter on the 15th), Herbert Haas (also a Beaufighter on the 15th), Dieter Schlief (Blenheim at night on the 18th) and finally Peter Laufs again (Hurricane on the 19th). All three pilots were from 1. *Staffel*.

Looking somewhat out of place sat in the broiling Libyan sunshine, this Ju 88C-4/C-6 of 2./NJG 2 was photographed at Benghazi in late 1941/early 1942. Finished in standard all-black nocturnal camouflage, the aircraft has the *Englandblitz* insignia beneath the cockpit. It seems that the only concession made to the *Staffel's* new theatre of operations is the white half-band applied to the rear fuselage. All Luftwaffe aircraft in the Mediterranean were supposed to be marked with a white band that fully encircled the rear fuselage. Finally, the aircraft's codes would have been applied in toned-down red (*Author's collection*)

Positive identification of who they had shot down is hard to reconcile, for RAF records for this period are incomplete and German records sometimes disagree on some of the dates.

However, the engagement on 19 December is clearer. That morning, three aircraft from 1./NJG 2 took off from Catania with orders to orbit Malta for about an hour. It is possible that Laufs shot down Plt Off Edward Steele of Hurricane-equipped No 126 Sqn over Grand Harbour, for he was later reported missing – but not before possibly having caused damage to Laufs' Ju 88C-2. A second aircraft, flown by Leutnant Wilhelm Brauns, was intercepted by four Hurricanes of No 249 Sqn led by Battle of Britain pilot Sqn Ldr Edward Mortimer-Rose. Despite trying to hide in cloud, Brauns was shot down by Mortimer-Rose, crashing at Bin Gemma on the island of Gozo. Brauns and his gunner bailed out wounded while the Bordfunker was killed.

The final losses for the year were Feldwebel Ernst Ziebarth of 2./NJG 2, who failed to return from an intruder mission to Malta on 22 December, and Leutnant Wilfried Babinek of 3./NJG 2 six days later. The latter had approached Malta at around 1940 hrs, dropped his bombs on the landing strip at Qrendi and then remained in the area, flying at low-level until his Ju 88C suffered a direct hit by light anti-aircraft fire. It exploded upon crashing on the western perimeter of the airfield at Hal Far, killing all three crew on board.

The first victory of 1942 went to *Gruppenkommandeur* Hauptmann Rolf Jung when he was credited with a Blenheim south of Malta on 4 January. Two more claims were made on the 23rd over a convoy for a Beaufighter by Leutnant Georg Wiedow of *Stab* I./NJG 2 and a Swordfish by Oberfeldwebel Hermann Sommer of 2./NJG 2 (his 11th victory).

However, three aircraft and their crews were lost on operations in January. The first of these involved Leutnant Dieter Schlief, now with 4./NJG 2, who crashed for unknown reasons at Ghar Mundu on Malta on the night of the 17th. Apparently one of ten aircraft carrying out intruder

Groundcrew load 50 kg bombs into a Ju 88C-4 of I./NJG 2 at an austere site somewhere in the North African theatre in 1942. Note the aircraft's codes are no longer toned down, with both the 'R4' (NJG 2's aircraft code) and the fuselage cross being clearly visible. Although deemed to be fighters first and foremost, Ju 88Cs routinely carried bombs to drop on targets (primarily airfields) during night intruder missions (*Author's Collection*)

sorties, Schlief's Ju 88C flew into a hillside close to the wreckage of a No 59 Sqn Hudson that had suffered the same fate earlier that night. Witnesses reported that the German aircraft was seen to be smoking prior to the crash, which killed its crew.

The following night, Leutnant Herbert Haas of 1./NJG 2 failed to return from a mission (in addition to his normal crew, he was also carrying a war reporter). Finally, on 26 January, the experienced Leutnant Peter Laufs of 1./NJG 2 crashed for unknown reasons near Adrano/Santuzza, 26 km northwest of Catania. Again, he and his crew were all killed. On 24 April Laufs was posthumously awarded the German Cross in Gold.

An idea of what I./NJG 2 was doing in the Mediterranean is clearly shown by the Flugbuch of Feldwebel Vincenz Giessübel of 2./NJG 2. He arrived at Catania at the start of January 1942 and flew his first mission – a night intruding sortie to Malta – on the 16th. His next operation saw him return there on 5 February, but on the night of the 6th he flew a convoy escort from Castel Benito, in Libya. This was then followed by a day convoy escort on 7 February, before Giessübel returned to Catania the following day. One more daylight convoy escort then took place on 15 February, and the following day he performed a daylight search mission. Giessübel's final operation in February was another night intruder mission to Malta on the 26th.

Curiously, some records credit Giessübel with a Beaufighter on 15 February, but no mention is made in his Flugbuch. However, the following day, Oberfeldwebel Hermann Jung of 2. *Staffel* and Leutnant Robert von Keudell of 4. *Staffel* each claimed a Wellington. Von Keudell would go missing east of Sicily on the night of 17 February, and he his crew were destined to be the last losses (and claimants, for that matter)

Luftwaffe officers in tropical uniform walk away from an all-black Ju 88C-6 nightfighter of 1./NJG 2 at Derna in early 1942. The officer on the left holding a camera is possibly either *Gruppenadjutant* Oberleutnant Hans Schulz or ace Oberleutnant Albert Hans Schulz. The *Gruppe*'s aircraft shifted bases regularly as, in addition to operating as fighters, they undertook convoy escort missions and reconnoitred for submarines (*EN Archive*)

for 4./NJG 2, as on 25 February the *Staffel* returned to the Netherlands to be part of the newly formed II./NJG 2.

March 1942 would prove to be a quieter month, with no victories recorded. The only casualties were due to accidents, with *Gruppenadjutant* Oberleutnant Hans Schulz being killed off Catania on the 8th, Unteroffizier Wolfgang Teuber of 1./NJG 2 crashing at Benghazi on the 17th and Leutnant Alfred Müller of *Stab* I./NJG 2 being lost at Catania on the 26th – there were no survivors from any of these Ju 88Cs. Feldwebel Giessübel flew three daylight convoy escorts in March from both Catania and Benghazi and two night intruder missions over Malta.

April would follow a similar pattern. Just one victory was claimed, by Oberfeldwebel Hermann Sommer of 2. *Staffel* (a Wellington on the 29th), and the new *Gruppenadjutant*, Leutnant Dieter Voigt, was killed in an accident off Augusta on the 21st. More worrying for I./NJG 2 was the loss on 8 April of the Ju 88A-4 Trop flown by Oberfeldwebel Alfred Vogel of 3./NJG 2, the aircraft having been shot down at night while operating over Malta by a Beaufighter of No 89 Sqn flown by Flt Lt Gilbert Hayton, with Plt Off Norman Joslin as his radar operator. The aircraft crashed at Huttaf Gandolf, near the Maltese village of Kirkop, killing all four crew.

April 1942 was a much busier month for Oberfeldwebel Giessübel, flying intruder missions to Malta on six occasions (6, 7, 9 10, 12 and 20 April), convoy escorts by day and night on 16, 18, 22 (twice) and 28 April and unspecified daylight missions from Benghazi, Derna (in Libya) and Catania on 27 April.

April 1942 would also see the arrival of the first Ju 88C-6s in-theatre for I./NJG 2.

On 4 May, the *Gruppe* achieved a notable first. At 1830 hrs, a Liberator of No 108 Sqn flown by Flt Lt Duncan McArthur lifted off from Fayid, in Egypt, to attack shipping off Tripoli. The bomber's observer, Flt Lt Phil Camp, described what happened next;

'0345hrs 4 May attacked by Ju 88 15 miles north of Benghazi. Rear Gunner Flt Sgt Denis Clifford killed. Petrol tanks punctured and fire started amidships but extinguished. All bomb releases u/s. Attempted to open bomb hatch manually. Second attack 2nd pilot killed (Plt Off Ivan Perkins). Aircraft on fire out of control. WOp Plt Off Douglas Hudson bailed out but caught parachute on escape hatch. Released. Gp Capt Faulkner May and Fg Off Leslie Speller bailed out from amidships. Self bailed out but captured in Arab tent 0900hrs on 4 May by Italians. Flt Lt McArthur found dead in wreck, parachute half open. Gp Capt May died of burns [22 May 1942]. Plt Off Hudson found dead. Fg Off Speller captured.'

The successful German pilot was Hauptmann Heinz Harmstorf, *Staffelkapitän* of 2./NJG 2, who recorded the following account for his second victory of the war;

'On the night of 3–4 May 1942 I flew a nightfighter sortie in the Benghazi area. At 0158hrs my Bordfunker Unteroffizier Krogill called, "A 4-engined aircraft over us!" I immediately turned towards the enemy aeroplane and recognised a Consolidated Liberator because of the four engines and the twin fins.

'I started my first attack, flying a bit lower, from left behind, and opened fire from about 150m. The burst hit the left wing and the fuselage and resulted in ammunition exploding in the rear of the fuselage – a fire broke out. The fire immediately went out again.

'Now the enemy dived away at high speed, and I needed about ten minutes until I was back in firing distance again. Just before I could begin my second attack, the enemy aircraft suddenly turned away so that I came behind his fuselage. Shortly after, the aeroplane sprayed out a sticky liquid that smeared the front window and reduced my view so that I could only recognise the aircraft by the exhaust flames. Immediately, I moved higher, but even several metres above the enemy aircraft the cockpit windows were smeared up even further.

'Now I gave a second burst of fire, which set on fire the right wing. The enemy descended with its burning wing and eventually exploded on impact. The fire could be observed for a long time.'

For Oberfeldwebel Giessübel, May 1942 would be his busiest month to date, with him noting ten escort missions from Catania, Derna and Tobruk (in Libya), an intruder mission to Malta on the 4th and another to Egypt on the 18th in his Flugbuch. His last sortie for the month was from Crete, flying from Heraklion on 23 May, after which he did not log a flight for just over two months.

In addition to Harmstorf's Liberator on 4 May, Oberfeldwebel Alfons Köster of 3./NJG 2 claimed two Blenheims north of Derna on the 12th and Oberleutnant Albert Schulz of 1. *Staffel* downed a Boston on the 31st. Two aircraft fell to anti-aircraft fire (one of which was the first C-6 to be lost by I./NJG 2), with one crewman wounded and the others killed. May also saw nine pilots posted in, one of whom, Leutnant Heinz Rökker, who joined 1. *Staffel*, would go on to claim 64 aircraft and be awarded the Knight's Cross with Oak Leaves.

June 1942 would be a busier month, with ten aircraft claimed to have been shot down. Four of these were credited to Leutnant Rökker, but in shooting down his first (a Beaufort of No 217 Sqn flown by Flg Off Frank Minster off Crete on the 20th) and his fourth (a Wellington on the 28th), his Ju 88C-6 was damaged in the first action and he crash-landed on fire, with all three crew wounded, after the second engagement. His wounds were not serious, for he was soon flying again operationally. Rökker's victory on 28 June was almost certainly the Wellington of No 108 Sqn flown by Sqn Ldr Donald Jacklin. One of ten aircraft briefed to undertake a night attack on German troop concentrations in the Mersa Matruh area of Egypt, No 108 Sqn's Operations Record Book (ORB) detailed what happened;

'Aircraft C was attacked by a Ju 88 and came under fire from this aircraft over a period of approximately 15 minutes, after which the Captain was able to manoeuvre the aircraft in such a way that the Front Gunner got in a 500-round burst and started a fire in the enemy aircraft. Following this, Sqn Ldr Jacklin disengaged and flew his aircraft to Amriya, where he was able to land on his wheels; the Wellington was badly damaged by the enemy fire, the rear turret being shot out of action and numerous other damage being done by both machine gun and cannon fire. This aircraft could not be flown away and was therefore taken over by 57 Repair and Salvage Unit. As a result of this engagement, a recommendation has been forwarded in respect of Sqn Ldr Jacklin.'

Leutnant Heinz Rökker (seen here as a Hauptmann after the award of the Oak Leaves to the Knight's Cross on 12 March 1945 for his 60th victory) was one of the first Mediterranean nightfighter aces of I./NJG 2. Having joined 1. *Staffel* in May 1942 after completing his training, he claimed six enemy bombers (five Wellingtons, one of which was not confirmed, and a Beaufort) shot down between 20 June 1942 and 19 April 1943. They were the first victories in Rökker's eventual tally of 61 confirmed kills (*Author's collection*)

The Wellington's main spar had been severed, pitot head shot away, starboard engine hit by cannon fire, starboard petrol tanks holed by cannon fire and hydraulics shot away. The starboard tyre had been punctured and, on landing, both engines caught fire.

Rökker reported the action as follows;

'At 2358hrs we discovered a Wellington and I attacked it at once from behind, and the right engine started to burn. The Wellington then suddenly flew very slowly and the pilot pushed the aircraft's nose steeply downwards. At once I reduced the throttles of my engines to stay behind and to start a second attack, but my speed was too great and I flew abeam of the Wellington at the same altitude.

'At that moment we saw the muzzle flash of the front gunner and heard the bullets hitting our aircraft. One bullet shattered in our cabin on the weapons panel and I was hurt by splinters above my right eye and in my right thigh. My Bordfunker was hurt by a splinter in his foot. But I did not give up the chase. At the same time we drew much closer to the ground, where I could clearly see vehicles in the bright moonlight. Some 100m further away the Wellington made a belly landing. I pulled my aircraft upwards again in order to look for more targets but my Bordmechaniker told me that the temperature of the right engine was rising and I had to cut the engine in order to avoid a fire.

'After I had finally managed to feather the propeller and to cut the engine, the left engine suddenly started burning. There were two alternatives – either we had to jump or we had to risk a belly landing at night. I decided

Oberleutnant Heinz Rökker's Ju 88C-6 of 1./NJG 2 in the Mediterranean in 1943. This aircraft is fitted with FuG 202 *Lichtenstein* AI radar – it also has a pair of 20 mm cannon fitted in its ventral gondola, with the barrel of the weapon on the right side being clearly visible. The Ju 88C-6 has had Maander camouflage paint hastily applied (*Author's collection*)

on the latter because we were at an altitude of just 300m. Shortly before hitting the ground, I gave the order to jettison the cabin roof; I pulled on the yoke so that we contacted the ground tail first.'

Although the aircrew of I./NJG 2 did not know it, July would be their last month of operations in the Mediterranean in 1942. It would be a busy one, with operations bringing mixed fortunes.

Between 4–6 July, Hauptmann Paul Semrau, *Staffelkapitän* of 3./NJG 2, claimed three Wellingtons, Leutnant Georg Wiedow of *Stab* I./NJG 2 two, and one each for Feldwebel Werner Heyne of 1./NJG 2 and Hauptmann Heinz Harmstorf of 2./NJG 2. However, Leutnant Erwin Wolfbauer of 3./NJG 2 was killed on 5 July when he crashed near RAF El Daba, in Egypt, after combat with a Wellington (possibly the aircraft from No 37 Sqn flown by Sgt Bob Withers). The following night Leutnant Georg Wiedow crashed whilst possibly attacking a Wellington of No 108 Sqn flown by Flt Sgt John Metcalfe, who duly reported;

'Aircraft L after bombing went to coast to pinpoint location, and immediately aircraft was attacked from starboard quarter by Ju 88 firing cannon. Violent evasive action was taken, and after a pause, it was hoped the attack was broken off. During this attack the Rear Gunner got in two bursts. A second attack was made by the enemy aircraft almost immediately and the Wellington was hit in several places.

'The Captain, in an endeavour to shake off the Ju 88, dived with violent evasive action, but was followed with continuous fire from the attacking aircraft, several shells bursting inside the fuselage. The Wellington was pulled out of the dive at 70ft, and although the controls had been jammed, the aircraft answered and climbed. At that moment there was a violent flash outside the Wellington, which momentarily died down, and was followed by a second flash. It is believed that the Ju 88, intent on keeping up the attack, did not pull out in time and crashed. After this there was no further attack.

'During the course of this engagement, the Wellington suffered the following damage: rear turret shot about, hydraulics rendered unserviceable (with the exception of the emergency landing gear), rudder control jammed, starboard main wheel punctured by machine gun bullets and sundry other damage. The aircraft was flown back as far as [RAF] Abu Sueir [in Egypt] before being put down; it was landed there on its wheels,

Some standard *Kampfgeschwader* also operated Ju 88C-6s in the Mediterranean, albeit in very limited numbers. This aircraft, for example, is from 9./KG 76, which was in-theatre from November 1942 through to July 1943, during which time it had a maximum of five Ju 88C-6s. F1+KT seen here was routinely flown by Hauptmann Dieter Lukesch, *Staffelkapitän* of 9./KG 76, from Catania, on Sicily, in May 1943. A veteran, and highly decorated, Ju 88 pilot, he would end the war flying Ar 234 jet bombers (*Author's collection*)

but owing to the burst tyre, the aircraft swung sharply shortly after landing, sheering off both port and starboard undercarriages.

'During the combat, the Wireless Operator (Sgt G A Arnold) was mortally wounded.'

There were no survivors from both German losses.

With the *Gruppe* kept busy escorting ships and resupplying Ju 52/3ms, the next victory did not occur until 20 July, when Oberfeldwebel Alfons Köster of 3./NJG 2 claimed a Maryland. Ten days earlier, Leutnant Wolfgang Wenning was forced to ditch off Crete after he suffered engine failure. Although he and his crew were quickly rescued, on the 20th his aircraft was reported missing during a daylight escort mission for Ju 52/3ms. There were no reported RAF claims and, this time, the crew did not survive.

The following night, Oberfeldwebel Alfons Köster crashed after combat with a Wellington near El Alamein, in Egypt. He and his crew trekked for a day-and-a-half before reaching German lines. Their opponent was possibly a No 40 Sqn aircraft flown by Plt Off P Greenway, which reported being attacked by a Ju 88 during a mission that saw German vehicles targeted 15–20 miles southwest of El Alamein.

On the night of 22 July, another No 40 Sqn Wellington was attacked three times by a Ju 88 while bombing the same target, leaving the rear turret badly damaged. Sgt R King managed to return to RAF Shallufa, in Egypt, but he crashed after overshooting the runway. Rear gunner Sgt Allan Macaskill was killed, but not before he almost certainly mortally wounded his attacker, Hauptmann Heinz Harmstorf. The German pilot was credited with a Wellington at 2250 hrs, but then received a fatal wound to his head from a burst of gunfire from the bomber. His Bordmechaniker, Unteroffizier Cornel Schiffbänker, although wounded himself, managed to land the damaged Ju 88C-6 at Haggag el Qasaba, in Egypt.

A further five victories would be claimed by month-end, taking the *Gruppe*'s tally to more than 40 victories while operating over the Mediterranean and North Africa. Its last claim was made by Oberfeldwebel Alfred Sievert of 2./NJG 2 for a Boston on 31 July. The *Gruppe*'s last loss in-theatre was a Ju 88C-6 of 3. *Staffel* that was destroyed in an accident on 4 August.

Two days earlier, I./NJG 2 had been ordered to transfer to Belgium, and in preparation, it had to assemble at Brindisi, in Italy, on 5 August. The *Gruppe* then flew to Melsbroek, in Belgium, where, after rest and recuperation, it was back in action over northwest Europe just over a month later. The first victory claimed from Melsbroek was a No 22 OTU Wellington flown by Sgt John Williams over Biervliet, in the Netherlands, on 10 September 1942, shot down by Oberleutnant Albert Schulz of 1. *Staffel* for his seventh claim of the war.

I./NJG 2 briefly returned to the Mediterranean in November 1942 following the Allied landings in Morocco and Algeria during Operation *Torch*. The *Gruppe* moved to Cazaux, in southwest France, on 8 November and then to Lézignan-Corbières, near Narbonne, eight days later as part of the short-lived German response codenamed Operation *Stockdorf*. I./NJG 2's subsequent return to Melsbroek shortly thereafter marked the end of Ju 88C operations over the Mediterranean for the time being.

Photographed here in late 1942 after he had received the Knight's Cross, Oberfeldwebel (later Hauptmann) Alfons Köster was credited with 11 night intruder victories over England while flying with I./NJG 2, followed by five more in the Mediterranean. He then moved to I./NJG 1, III./NJG 2, 9./NJG 2 and, finally, 12./NJG 3. Köster, having taken his tally to 20 victories, was killed on 7 January 1945 while serving as *Staffelkapitän* of IV./NJG 3 when his Ju 88G collided with the roof of a farmhouse in fog close to Varel-Obenstrohe airfield in Germany (*Author's Collection*)

COLOUR PLATES

1
Ju 88C-0 Wk-Nr 0096 CN+NR of Z.St./KG 30, Ludwigslust, Germany, spring 1940

2
Ju 88C-2 G9+CM of 4./NJG 1, Düsseldorf, Germany, June 1940

3
Ju 88C-1 Wk-Nr 0142 4D+MH of Z.St./KG 40, Stavanger, Norway, June 1940

4
Ju 88C-4 Wk-Nr 0343 R4+CH of 1./NJG 2, Gilze-Rijen, the Netherlands, March 1941

42

5
Ju 88C-4 R4+MT of *Ergänzungs/NJG 2*, Gilze-Rijen, the Netherlands, spring 1942

6
Ju 88C-4 R4+WK of 2./NJG 2, Benghazi, Libya, summer 1942

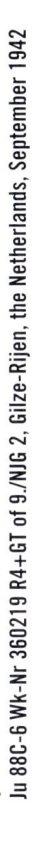

7
Ju 88C-6 Wk-Nr 360219 R4+GT of 9./NJG 2, Gilze-Rijen, the Netherlands, September 1942

8 Ju 88C-6 Wk-Nr 360008 3U+KU of 10./ZG 26, Trapani, Sicily, April 1943

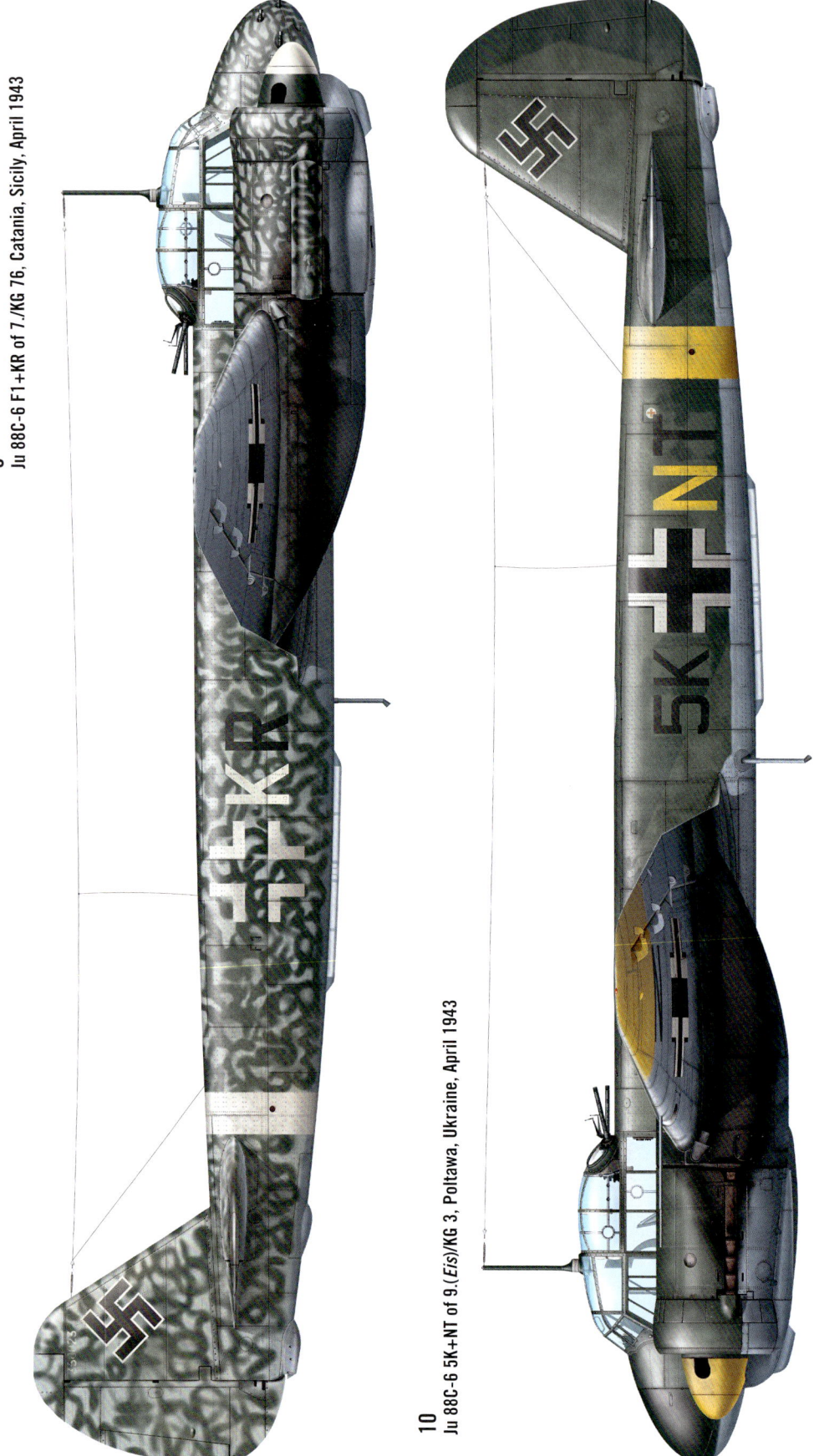

9
Ju 88C-6 F1+KR of 7./KG 76, Catania, Sicily, April 1943

10
Ju 88C-6 5K+NT of 9.(*Eis*)/KG 3, Poltawa, Ukraine, April 1943

11
Ju 88C-6 9K+HR of 7./KG 51, Bagerovo, Ukraine, spring 1943

12
Ju 88C-6 F8+HX of 13./KG 40, Cognac, France, spring 1943

13
Ju 88C-6 Wk-Nr 360063 F8+EZ of 15./KG 40, Lorient, France, spring 1943

14
Ju 88C-6 F8+DY of 14./KG 40, Bordeaux-Mérignac, France, summer 1943

15
Ju 88C-6 F8+MZ of 15./KG 40, Bordeaux-Mérignac, France, summer 1943

16
Ju 88C-6 D5+EX of IV./NJG 3, Karup, Denmark, summer 1943

17
Ju 88C-6 Wk-Nr 750370 3U+GU of 10./ZG 26, Eleusis, Greece, August 1943

18
Ju 88C-6 F8+YZ of 15./KG 40, Bordeaux-Mérignac, France, autumn 1943

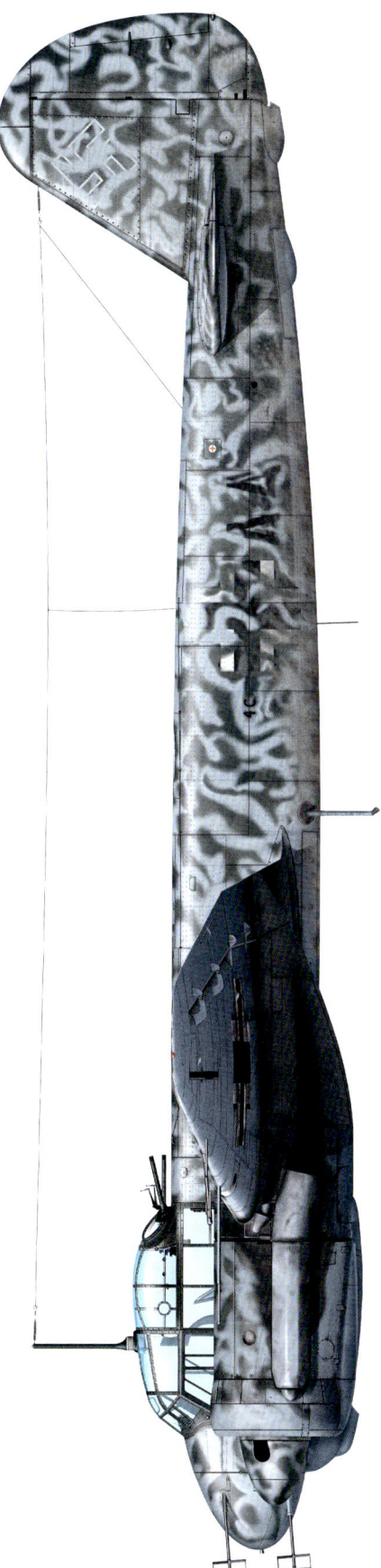

19
Ju 88C-6 4C+AA of *Sonderkommando Kunkel*, Bordeaux-Mérignac, France, November 1943

20
Ju 88C-6 R4+KP of 6./NJG 2, Kassel-Rothwesten, Germany, May 1944

CHAPTER FOUR

10. AND 11./ZG 26

On 4 September 1942, the Allies confirmed from German sources the departure of I./NJG 2 from the Mediterranean. It was also ascertained that the *Gruppe* had left 26 of its Ju 88Cs behind, seven of which would be assigned to 10./ZG 26 at Derna. These changes had first been picked up by the Allies on 22 August when signals traffic indicated Ju 88C-6s Wk-Nrs 360007 and 360008 and Ju 88C-4 Wk-Nr 249 were being allocated to 10./ZG 26 at Haggag el Qasaba from Generalfeldmarschall Albert Kesselring's *Luftflotte* 2 reserve held at Foggia, in Italy.

10. *Staffel* had been formed in March 1942 with eight Do 17Zs. Based in Crete, it was tasked with escorting convoys between Greece and Crete, predominantly in daylight. The unit suffered a single loss when, on 18 June, a Do17Z-2 ditched off the Libyan coast following engine failure. The replacement of the Do 17s with Ju 88C-6s began in September, and within two months all the Dorniers had gone.

10./ZG 26 was commanded by 31-year-old Hauptmann Peter Habicht. An experienced pre-war civilian flying instructor, he had first joined Bf 110-equipped 7./ZG 26 in the autumn of 1941. Injured in an accident on 8 November when his Bf 110 suffered engine failure and he ditched in the Mediterranean off Spartivento, Italy, Habicht joined 8./ZG 26 after his recovery. He claimed his first victory – a B-17 off Malta – on 22 February 1942. This is believed to have been the aircraft from No 220 Sqn flown by Flg Off Fred Stokes that reported being attacked by two Bf 110s while searching

The pilot of Ju 88C-6 3U+OU of 10./ZG 26 flies in close formation with his section leader at the end of a late afternoon patrol (possibly from Derna) over the Mediterranean. Neither 10. or 11./ZG 26 undertook nightfighter operations with their Ju 88C-6s (*Family–Archiv Seidelmann/ Author's collection*)

for the Italian fleet, but which returned undamaged, albeit claiming to have shot down one of the Messerschmitts. Habicht was promoted to Hauptmann in April 1942, and two months later took command of 10./ZG 26.

The first recorded Ju 88C loss for 10. *Staffel* occurred at Derna on 7 September when a Ju 88C-4 crashed, not as a result of combat, killing Unteroffizier Gerhard Franze and two crew. The first combat loss occurred on 12 October when battle-damaged Ju 88C-6 Wk-Nr 360232 was force-landed by Feldwebel Hugo Brückner at Ain el-Gazala, in Libya. The pilot and one crewman were wounded.

On 19 November, two Ju 88Cs were involved in combat with what were believed to be Kittyhawks of No 250 Sqn ten miles off the coast from the Libyan airfield of Martuba. Flg Offs Gordon Troke and James Collier each claimed a Ju 88 destroyed, with a third example possibly damaged. 10./ZG 26 reported one of its Ju 88s being shot down east of Apollonia, in Libya, and a second aircraft returned to Sidi el-Magrun, again in Libya, only to crash on landing. Leutnant Theodor Schuster and his crew were reported missing from the former aircraft, while the latter, flown by the unlucky Feldwebel Hugo Brückner, had two crew killed. The pilot escaped unscathed.

The first, and as it would transpire, only air combat claim for the *Staffel* came on 25 October. Two Ju 88C-6s that were about to take up the escort of a tanker off Tobruk reported a combat with two Beaufighters, and Hauptmann Peter Habicht claimed to have shot one of them down. He wrote the following report;

'On 25 October 1942 at 1115 hrs I had the first success of the *Staffel* with the Ju 88. During an escort mission north of Tobruk I was engaged in a 20-minute air battle with two Beaufighters which wanted to attack the ships we were protecting. I managed to shoot down one of them, which hit the sea with a huge splash; the other aircraft quickly fled.'

It is believed that what Habicht actually shot down was a Beaufort flown by Flg Off Richard Bendwig of No 1 Overseas Aircraft Despatch Unit (OADU) probably en route to join No 47 Sqn at RAF Gianaclis, in Egypt, from Malta, the clue coming from Air HQ Malta's Diary entry for 25 October 1942, which stated;

'Arrivals – two Spitfires, one Hudson, one Liberator from Gibraltar, one DC-3 from LG 224 [Cairo West]. Departures – two Beauforts, one DC-3 to LG 224. Aircraft casualties – one Spitfire failed to return to base, pilot missing [Plt Off Nigel Park of No 126 Sqn was probably shot down by Lt Alfred Hammer of 4./JG 53]; one Beaufort missing in transit between Malta and LG 224, believed shot down by enemy aircraft, crew missing.'

It would appear that the Beauforts had the misfortune to meet up with 10./ZG 26, and the '20-minute air battle' was in fact both RAF aircraft trying to get away, only one of which did.

For the next five months, 10./ZG 26 appears to have carried out its business without incident. By means of example, Feldwebel Hermann Bolten had been involved with tactical trials of the Me 210 with the *Erprobungsstaffel* 210 from July 1942, and at the end of October he flew to the Mediterranean for further operational trials with

The final moments of the Beaufort flown by Flg Off Richard Bendwig of No 1 OADU, downed by the *Staffelkapitän* of 10./ZG 26, Hauptmann Peter Habicht, on 25 October 1942 (*Family–Archiv Seidelmann/Author's collection*)

this aircraft. His unit was now designated 16./KG 6, and it was subordinate to 10./ZG 26. He flew his first mission – a convoy escort from Kastelli, on Crete – on 4 November.

After 18 operational flights over the Mediterranean in the Me 210, Bolten then flew a Ju 88C-6 from Chinisia, on Sicily, on 18 January 1943 with 10./ZG 26, his aircraft being coded 3U+KU. He would undertake a total of 19 operational flights in the Ju 88, all of them daylight ship or convoy escorts, before returning to Germany after 6 February to join the *Erprobungsstaffel* Me 410 at Lechfeld.

The *Bordschütze* of the lead Ju 88C-6 took this photograph of four other aircraft from 10./ZG 26 flying over the Mediterranean in loose formation during early 1943. The *Staffel* usually had around 18 Ju 88C-6s on strength at this time, typically flying them on missions from Sicily and Crete (*Family– Archiv Seidelmann/Author's collection*)

By April 1943, 10./ZG 26 had an establishment of 18 aircraft, but at any one time just half of them were serviceable.

The first combat loss of the year came on 20 April when Ju 88C-6 Wk-Nr 360009 (one of the original aircraft transferred to the *Staffel* in August 1942 from I./NJG 2) was reported shot down 50 km west of the island of Marettimo, west of Sicily, after combat with 'P-51s', killing Unteroffizier Hans Köhler and his crew. They were probably shot down northwest of Cap Bon, in Tunisia, by 2Lt John P Bedford and Capt Fred A Borsodi of the P-40 Warhawk-equipped 86th Fighter Squadron (FS)/79th Fighter Group (FG). However, there were also other claims made that same day for Ju 88s destroyed by No 112 Sqn and No 2 Sqn South African Air Force (five miles off Ras el Mar), the successful South African

Ju 88C-6 Wk-Nr 750370 3U+GU assigned to 10./ZG 26 has its engines run up on Crete under the watchful gaze of both air- and groundcrew. This aircraft crashed following a collision with another Ju 88C-6 from the *Staffel* on 25 August 1943. Both crews were killed in the incident (*Family–Archiv Seidelmann/Author's collection*)

pilots being Capt L C H Hope and Lt G Oglivie Watson. The latter two units were equipped with Kittyhawks. A second Ju 88C-6 was also damaged whilst landing at Trapani following an operational mission on this date.

10./ZG 26 would suffer three more accidents before the end of June that resulted in the deaths of pilots Feldwebeln Franz Behringer (6th) and Wilhelm Heining (10th) and Oberfeldwebel Kurt Bonnemann (26th). Then on 25 August, the aircraft flown by Unteroffizier Otto Müller and Leutnant Wilhelm Debes collided near the island of Euboea east of Athens, in Greece, killing both crews.

10./ZG 26 had relocated to the Italian mainland in May, and in August half of the *Staffel* was withdrawn to Öttingen, in Germany. Here, it became 7./ZG 76 in November, at which point the unit re-equipped with Bf 110s. Hauptmann Peter Habicht would now command the remaining half, which became 11./ZG 26 based at Eleusis, in Greece. Habicht had been awarded the Honour Goblet of the Luftwaffe on 30 April 1943, and on 17 October he received the German Cross in Gold.

Notwithstanding the transfer of 10./ZG 26 back to Germany, on 16 May 1943, 11./ZG 26 was formed at Athens-Kalamaki using half of 10. *Staffel*'s Ju 88Cs, to which new aircraft were assigned, taking its establishment to a maximum of 11. The unit's primary task was also convoy escort between Greece and Crete and in the Aegean, but as the war turned more against Germany, a secondary role was considered to have been anti-partisan missions in Yugoslavia and Greece. No clear evidence has been found to indicate such sorties were flown, however.

11./ZG 26 moved to Athens-Eleusis in June, suffering its first casualties on the 27th of that month when two Ju 88C-6s were damaged during the bombing of the airfield by B-24s. The *Staffel* was involved in operations off the Greek islands of Kos, Leros and Samos from September 1943 onwards, losing its first aircraft and crew in the Aegean on the 18th when Oberfeldwebel Heinz Gründling went missing off Rhodes.

September 1943 also saw Hauptmann Peter Habicht hand over the *Staffel* to Hauptmann Wilhelm Pflanz, another long-serving Bf 110 pilot with ZG 26. Habicht returned to Germany, where he took command of the *Ergänzungs Zerstörer Gruppe* based at Braunschweig-Broitzen. He was eventually shot down and killed in an Me 410A-1 on 11 January 1944 near Ottleben, having fallen victim to Lt Bob Stephens of the P-51B Mustang-equipped 354th FG.

Returning to 11./ZG 26, on 12 November 1943, Ju 88C-6s flown by Leutnant Hans Sukowski and Unteroffizier Gregor Merva failed to

Hauptmann Peter Habicht (left) checks the starboard propeller blades of a Ju 88C-6 from 10./ZG 26 during his pre-flight inspection. Habicht had previously flown Bf 110s prior to taking command of 10. and then 11./ZG 26. He was eventually killed in action at the controls of an Me 410 on 11 January 1944 whilst commanding the *Ergänzungs Zerstörer Gruppe* during operations in the defence of Germany (*Family–Archiv Seidelmann/Author's collection*)

return from operations off Leros. There were no Allied claims that matched up with these losses, despite four Beaufighters of No 47 Sqn and three B-25s of the 310th Bombardment Group (BG), escorted by six Beaufighters of No 603 Sqn, attacking a convoy off Leros during the afternoon of the 12th. Allied crews reported seeing German aircraft in the vicinity, but they made no mention of any combats with Ju 88s – Flg Off Athol Greentree of No 47 Sqn was shot down and killed, although his aircraft almost certainly fell to Flak.

Leutnant Hans Sukowski had only joined 11./ZG 26 on 23 October, having completed his training on the Ju 88C-6 with 10./KG 40 three days earlier. His first operational flight was a fighter sweep between Athens and Rhodes on the afternoon of 30 October. Following this mission he reported combat with two Beaufighters – probably those flown by WO Harry Nice and Sgt Elwyn James of No 227 Sqn – south of the island of Kastellorizo. Sukowski's death occurred on only his fourth operational flight.

Two claims were made by two unidentified NCO pilots from 11./ZG 26 on 16 November (the day that British troops surrendered on Leros) for two Beaufighters over the Aegean. That day, Nos 47 and 603 Sqns attacked a Siebel ferry off the island of Kalymnos that was carrying troops to reinforce Leros. As well as a surface escort, the ferry was also protected by seven Ar 196s, four Bf 109s and four Ju 88s. Despite hitting the ferry, which then caught fire and sank, Beaufighters flown by Flg Offs Bill Thwaites, Tony Bond and John Fletcher were shot down. Aside from the 11./ZG 26 claims, Bf 109s of III./JG 27 led by Major Ernst Düllberg claimed three Beaufighters in the Levita/Kos/Tría Nisiá area.

The new year saw 11./ZG 26 continuing to perform daylight convoy escort duties. In January, the unit reported just eight aircraft available. Although this number would rise to a maximum of 26 by May, just three aircraft would be lost in the first six months of 1944.

The first casualty came during the afternoon of 31 January when eight Beaufighters of No 252 Sqn, led by Battle of Britain pilot Flt Lt Reg Meyer, undertook an offensive shipping search in the eastern Aegean. When off the northern tip of the island of Stampalia they intercepted three Ju 88s, and Meyer (who was shot down and killed ten days later by III./JG 27) was credited with downing one of them. At the same time, the Beaufighter flown by Flg Off Darrell Hall was seen to crash into the sea close to where the Ju 88 had gone down. The 11. *Staffel* Ju 88C-6 was flown by Unteroffizier Franz Grüber, whose Bordfunker, Unteroffizier Friedrich Stoll, was credited with shooting down a Beaufighter before their own demise – all three German crew were killed.

One of the other German pilots involved, Unteroffizier Herbert Glöge, reported taking off from Gadurra, on the island of Rhodes, at 1300 hrs, bound for Stampalia. Once there, he engaged in combat with 'four Mitchells', one of which was shot down for the loss of a Ju 88. The surviving German aircraft landed at Eleusis at 1725 hrs, while the Beaufighter flown by Flt Sgt F A Stevenson force-landed in Turkey.

Staffelkapitän Hauptmann Wilhelm Pflanz was awarded the Honour Goblet of the Luftwaffe on 8 May, but shortly thereafter he is believed to have handed over command to Hauptmann Richard Riedel.

After four months without a loss, 11./ZG 26 suffered a double blow in the space of 24 hours. On 8 June, the Ju 88C-6 flown by Oberfeldwebel Heinrich Schiller crashed ten kilometres east of Cape Santa Maria di Leuca, in southern Italy. The following morning, Unteroffizier Günter König was reported missing on operations. Flt Lt Don Pinks and his navigator Flt Sgt Maurice Noble of Beaufighter-equipped No 255 Sqn were on an anti-reconnaissance patrol from Rosignano, in Italy, when they shot down a Ju 88 (possibly König's aircraft) off 'Cap Maria de Leuca' at 0427 hrs;

'Identified as Ju 88 or 188. Opened fire at 250yds with one-second burst almost dead astern. Saw strikes on engine, wing and fuselage. Port engine began to smoke and debris flew from starboard wing. Beaufighter's bulletproof windshield became covered with oil and second attack presented rather difficult sighting through this slick. Second attack delivered from 15 degrees port same level 200yds and registered strikes on engine and fuselage once more. Immediately, the already smoking port engine was followed by smoke from the starboard engine, and apparently dense black smoke was given out from the fuselage too.

'The enemy lost height very quickly, its nose dipped, and as we flew past its port side [we] identified it as a Ju 88. Turned to port for another attack if necessary, but during the turn the Navigator reported it had gone in and almost immediately sank.'

These would be the last operational losses suffered by 11./ZG 26, for at the start of September the *Staffel* was recalled from the Mediterranean. Its journey back to Germany was far from uneventful. On 2 September, a Ju 88C-6 crashed near Mauthausen, in Austria, on its way northwards, killing Unteroffizier Walter Baumann, two crew, an engineer and a passenger.

By 10 September, 23 Ju 88C-6s of 11./ZG 26 were reported being with *Luftflotte* 5 at Oerlandet, in Denmark. This number had been reduced to 16 by 20 November, despite few, if any, operational flights having been carried out during the autumn of 1944. November also saw 11. *Staffel* commence its conversion to the Me 410. Surplus Ju 88C-6s languished at Oerlandet until the end of February 1945, when all 16 surviving aircraft were assigned to reconnaissance unit *Fernaufklärungsstaffel* 1.(F)/*Aufklärungsgruppe* 120. Whether they were ever used in this new role remains unknown.

It has been suggested that in addition to daylight escort missions, 10. and 11./ZG 26 also carried out nightfighter operations. However, such sorties have not been found in the few logbooks that have surfaced since 1945. For example, Unteroffizier Herbert Glöge joined 10./ZG 26 at Gerbini, on Sicily, at the start of March 1943, flying his first mission (a daylight convoy escort) on 4 April, after which he flew daylight escort sorties or sea reconnaissance until 26 July. In December Glöge joined 11./ZG 26, after which he undertook exactly the same types of missions until returning to Germany on 1 September 1944, his last flight being from Oerlandet to Gardermoen on 11 November.

Photographed in Sicily in 1943, Ju 88C-6 3U+GU of 10./ZG 26 featured the ZG 26 insignia on its nose (*Author's collection*)

CHAPTER FIVE

TRAIN-BUSTING

A number of *Kampfgeschwader* operated the Ju 88C-6 on the Eastern Front. In most units, the precise roles these aircraft performed remains unclear, apart from tricking Soviet fighter pilots into thinking they were attacking vulnerable bombers as opposed to heavily armed fighters. This could be best illustrated by the fact that some units painted glazed bomber noses over the solid noses of their Ju 88C-6s, further adding to the ruse. However, a number of units flying Ju 88C-6s used them in the interdiction role against Soviet trains and railway lines well behind the frontline.

In April 1942, Feldwebel Gerhard Rasch was posted from Ju 88-equipped 10./KG 3 at Mons, in Belgium, to 6./KG 3 on the Eastern Front, flying his first mission with his new *Staffel* on the 19th. In addition to normal bombing missions, some pilots in II./KG 3 performed what Rasch called 'unusual duties';

'*Staffelkapitän* Hauptmann Peter Breu and Oberfeldwebel Wolfgang Martin were engaged in train-busting experiments with the Ju 88C and Ju 88P. Leutnant Ferdinand Zimmermann, who had risen from the ranks, and Unteroffizier Helmut Rösner often joined in train-strafing missions, and I too became a member of this unit-within-a-unit. On 21 May 1942, I flew high cover as Hauptmann Breu attacked a train south of Kharkov. Two Ratas managed to cling to Breu's tail and I dived vertically at one in the hope of scaring him off. A quick burst of 20mm cannon and the Soviet fighter exploded in a dirty grey puff of smoke.'

This Ju 88C-6 from an unidentified unit on the Eastern Front was made to look as if it was a normal Ju 88A bomber by the painting of what appeared to be a Perspex bomber nose. This unit-applied measure of deception appeared on a number of C-6s operating against the Soviet transport network (*Author's collection*)

For 6./KG 3, train-busting operations were performed in addition to its normal bombing attacks. II. *Gruppe* reported receiving its first five Ju 88C-6s to fly alongside 20 Ju 88A-4s in May 1942. By July it had eight train-busters, but from September the unit only had two and by December it had none.

Undertaking such missions was hazardous. On 14 June 1942, Rasch was returning from his 64th operational sortie that had seen him targeting trains in the Velikiye–Luki-Nelidovo area when he lost an engine after it had been hit by anti-aircraft fire. He crash-landed Ju 88C-6 Wk-Nr 360185 5K+BP near a small town some 320 km behind the frontline, which shows how deeply these train-busters penetrated into enemy territory. Rasch, his Beobachter Unteroffizier Otto Wirth and Bordfunker Obergefreiter Gerhard Guth managed to get out of their burning aeroplane, but this was only the start of a traumatic series of events, as Rasch subsequently recalled;

'We were quickly brought to our senses by the sound of shouting from the nearby village. A mob of screaming women and children were rushing towards us. Terror gave us the power to run towards a river some kilometres away, but the Russians closed the gap. Guth fell behind and was beaten to death by the mob. His screams followed us as we reached the river and plunged in. Swimming across, we continued our flight.

'Living on bark, berries and frogs, we slowly made our way west but the strain became so great that Wirth began to go out of his mind, and on the seventh day after the crash he tried to shoot me. Just as I wrestled the Luger from Wirth's demented grip, a man emerged from a nearby wood. We both threw ourselves to the ground as the man approached. He began to plough, and after some time I realised it was a German soldier augmenting his rations.'

Rasch would go on to complete 287 operational flights, and was credited with destroying 45 trains (one of them armoured), 27 tanks and 200 trucks. He would be awarded the Honour Goblet of the Luftwaffe in October 1942, and although recommended for the Knight's Cross, only received the German Cross in Gold. Following a crash on 6 June 1943, Rasch was permanently removed from frontline flying, while Unteroffizier Otto Wirth never returned to operational duties.

In January 1943, two specialist Ju 88C-6 train-busting *Staffeln* were formed. III./KG 1 had handed its aircraft over to II./KG 1 when the *Gruppe* left for Königsberg-Neuhausen in East Prussia on 31 October 1942. During the refitting and re-equipping of III. *Gruppe*, 9./KG 1 received three Ju 88C-6s and was re-designated 9.(*Eisenbahn*)/ KG 1 to signify its new role as a train-buster unit. 9. *Staffel* also continued to fly Ju 88A-4s as well, and had returned to Dno, on the Eastern Front, by 24 January 1943.

The *Staffel's* first Ju 88C-6 loss came on 9 March when Wk-Nr 360297 flown by Unteroffizier Herbert Müller was shot down by fighters while attacking targets in the Morosovo–Ostaschkovo

A Ju 88C-6 of 9.(*Eis*)/KG 3 showing the *Kampfgeschwader's* lightning bolt insignia on the nose. This unit enjoyed notable success while operating a small number of C-6s against railway-related targets during the first six months of 1943 (*Author's collection*)

area. His Beobachter, Leutnant Rolf Hart, had received the Knight's Cross in October 1942 for completing 400 missions, the German Cross in Gold in April 1942 for 250 missions and, before that, the Honour Goblet of the Luftwaffe. Long-serving members of 9. *Staffel*, Hart and his crew were credited with the destruction of nine transport trains and two Soviet freighters prior to their deaths.

The only known *Staffelkapitän* of 9.(*Eis*)/KG 1 was Oberleutnant Alfred Siebert, who had received the Honour Goblet of the Luftwaffe in June 1942 and German Cross in Gold six months later. He would be badly injured in a crash on 7 July 1943, and his replacement is not known.

9.(*Eis*)/KG 1 continued to support Army Group North until June 1943 when it was transferred to *Luftflotte* 6. Prior to this, the *Staffel* had helped German forces hold the line after the Battle of Krasny Bor (10–13 February 1943), and then flew in the Volkhov, Kolpino and Kholm regions.

After joining *Luftflotte* 6, it was active during Operation *Citadel* (the German attack in the Kursk salient), which lasted from 5–17 July. III./KG 1 carried out bombing operations until it moved to Bryansk on 14 July, from where the *Gruppe* attacked Soviet armour that had advanced to Orel following the launching of Operation *Kutuzov* (the Soviet counteroffensive) on the 12th. On 20 July 9.(*Eis*)/KG 1 moved back to Seshchinskaya, and it would subsequently transfer to Stari Bykhov on 18 September. By then, the rest of III./KG 1 had left the Eastern Front, the *Gruppe* returning to Flensburg, in Germany, on 2 August to convert to the Ju 88P. By April 1944 it had disbanded.

9.(*Eis*)/KG 1 soldiered on in the east into October 1943, helping Army Group Centre contain the Red Army's Orsha offensives launched that

9.(*Eis*)/KG 3's *Staffelkapitän*, Oberleutnant Ernst Fach, is hoisted onto the shoulders of groundcrew at Poltawa in April 1943 upon the successful completion of 300 missions conducted against, or involving contact with, the enemy. His Ju 88C-6 can be seen behind, with the lightning bolt emblem of KG 3 on its nose. Also just visible to the right of the insignia is the 'wing' of the wing and train wheel badge of 9.(*Eis*)/KG 3. Fach was barred from further operational flying immediately after reaching the 300 missions mark, by which point he had destroyed 64 locomotives and nine complete goods trains (*Author's collection*)

autumn. Its last recorded Ju 88C-6 incident occurred on 19 October when Wk-Nr 750762 suffered slight damage from anti-aircraft fire over Torpotez. During its operations over the Eastern Front, the *Staffel* had lost just two aircraft in combat, on 9 March (flown by Unteroffizier Herbert Müller) and 13 July (flown by Oberfeldwebel Wilhelm Bischof).

9.(*Eis*)/KG 1 then departed for Flensburg to convert to the Ju 88P along with the rest of III. *Gruppe*. On 1 February 1944 it was re-designated 14.(*Eis*)/KG 3, and the *Staffel* (commanded by Oberleutnant Udo Cordes, formerly of 9.(*Eis*.)/KG 3, from 24 May 1944) would subsequently fly the Ju 88P for 12 months from March 1944.

To accompany 9.(*Eis*)/KG 1, 9.(*Eis*)/KG 3 was formed under the leadership of Hauptmann Otto Meichsner in early January 1943. Equipped with nine Ju 88C-6s, it was tasked with attacking the Soviet rail network in the Donets Basin. Meichsner, who had already been awarded the Honour Goblet of the Luftwaffe, would be killed on operations on 11 January (and duly awarded the German Cross Kreuz in Gold posthumously) while flying a Ju 88A-4.

Command of the *Staffel* now went to Oberleutnant Ernst Fach, formerly *Staffelkapitän* of 4./KG 3. He had transferred to the Luftwaffe from the Wehrmacht in 1933, becoming a bomber pilot. From September 1939 until May 1941, Fach flew Do 17s with 4./KG 3, during which time he became adept at making attacks on pinpoint targets such as airfields. Converting to the Ju 88, Fach joined 6./KG 3, and in the first months of Operation *Barbarossa* (the German invasion of the USSR in June 1941) he accounted for numerous tanks, artillery positions and bridges, as well as nine trains and a Soviet fighter. Fach's Ju 88A-4 was shot down over enemy territory on 26 March 1942, but he managed to return to German lines with his crew.

Records indicate that Fach took command of 6./KG 3 from Hauptmann Peter-Paul Breu (who became *Gruppenkommandeur* of II./KG 3) at the end of June 1942. Just two months later, Fach was made *Staffelkapitän* of 4./KG 3 after Hauptmann Hans Reinewald was wounded on 3 July. Finally, as previously noted, in January he was given command of 9.(*Eis*)/KG 3.

In a matter of weeks, the Ju 88C-6s of 9.(*Eis*)/KG 3 had claimed 216 Soviet trains destroyed, Fach being credited with 44 of them – a further 40 were also damaged. In April 1943, having completed 300 combat missions, Fach was barred from undertaking further operations. By then his score stood at 64 locomotives and nine complete goods trains destroyed.

That same month, the *Staffel*'s airfield at Zaparozhye-East was bombed and one of its Ju 88C-6s destroyed, forcing 9.(*Eis*)/KG 3 to move to Poltava. Tragedy struck near the unit's new home on 15 May when Fach's Ju 88C-6 crashed during a training flight, killing both him and his crew (Oberfeldwebel Walter Schmidt and Oberleutnant Wolfgang Siegel). Fach was posthumously awarded the Knight's Cross and promoted to Hauptmann on 3 September 1943.

Leutnant Udo Cordes was *Staffelkapitän* of 9.(*Eis*)/KG 3 from mid-1943. He joined 4./KG 3 in the spring of 1942, before transferring to 9.(Eis.)/KG 3 in January 1943, where he quickly proved himself to be a 'Lok-Töter' ('locomotive killer'). Indeed, he accounted for the destruction of 81 enemy locomotives, as well as many trains, stations and bridges. Awarded the Knight's Cross on 25 May 1943, Cordes had flown 296 combat missions by war's end. He is standing here before his Ju 88C-6, which carries both KG 3's emblem and the winged railway insignia of his *Staffel* (*Author's collection*)

His successor was Leutnant Udo Cordes, who had quickly developed a reputation as a 'Lok-Töter' ('locomotive killer'). Cordes joined II./KG 3 in the spring of 1942 and flew with both 4. and 6. *Staffeln* prior to being assigned to 9.(*Eis*)/KG 3 shortly after its establishment. Over a period of just three weeks, he and his crew destroyed 41 locomotives and 19 trains, including some single days where he accounted for several. Cordes' greatest successes came on 14 March 1943, when he destroyed five locomotives, and six engines and a fuel train three days later. He was awarded the Knight's Cross on 25 May 1943, by which time he had flown around 150 combat missions.

In June 1943, III./KG 3 moved from Poltava back to Germany to be retrained as a Beleuchter (illuminator) *Gruppe*, and it appears that 9.(*Eis*)/KG 3 was withdrawn at the same time. Throughout its six-month existence, the *Staffel* had reported a maximum establishment of nine Ju 88C-6s, and by April it was also flying Ju 88A-4s. 9.(*Eis*)/KG 3 had lost five aircraft in combat – on 20 February and 24 March (both flown by Feldwebel Erhardt Lehmann), 11 May (Oberfeldwebel Herbert Röwer) and two on 5 June (flown by Leutnant Jürgen Fricke and Unteroffizier Ernst Meyer – it is believed these aircraft collided).

Both Lehmann and Röwer were recipients of the Honour Goblet of the Luftwaffe and German Cross in Gold, while Röwer would be awarded the Knight's Cross posthumously after his death, having been credited with 59 locomotives, 14 complete trains, 18 tanks, 90 trucks and two Flak batteries destroyed and a further 11 locomotives and 25 tanks damaged.

As 6./KG 3's Feldwebel Rasch alluded to earlier in this chapter, other units aside from the specialist Ju 88C-6 train-busting *Staffeln* (9.(*Eis*)/KG 1 and 9.(*Eis*)/KG 3) also carried out such duties, but this was very much a secondary role for them. For example, 7./KG 51 was sometimes referred to as 7.(*Eis*)/KG 51 because in addition to its Ju 88A-4s, it had two Ju 88C-6s on strength in August–September 1942. Two more were flown in in April–May 1943, and by June of that year this number had risen to five. This increase coincided with Oberleutnant Hans Gutzmer taking command of 7. *Staffel*, after which it carried out dedicated train-busting missions in the Central Sector until the end of August when III./KG 51 returned to Germany. By year-end the *Gruppe* had been disbanded.

7./KG 51 lost two Ju 88C-6s during its limited association with the aircraft. Oberfeldwebel Walter Kase and his crew were captured on 26 April 1943 after force-landing with a technical problem and, two days later, Unteroffizier Leopold Hofmeister and his crew failed to return from a mission to Timoschewskaja-Jeisk.

It is therefore fair to say that 9.(*Eis*)/KG 1. and 9.(*Eis*)/KG 3 were the only Ju 88C-6-equipped units to exclusively perform the specialist train-busting role – a challenging mission they undertook exclusively on the Eastern Front for a maximum of just ten months.

Aircrew from 7./KG 51 sit around in the sunshine, possibly at Tazinskaja, between missions in August–September 1942. The Ju 88C-6 behind them (one of only two C-6s then assigned to the *Staffel*) has also had its solid nose painted to make it look like a normal Ju 88A bomber, more than 20 of which were then operated by 7. *Staffel* (*Author's collection*)

CHAPTER SIX

ZERSTÖRER OVER THE ATLANTIC

Relieved to see a Luftwaffe aircraft overhead rather than one from the RAF or USAAF, the crew of an unidentified Type VIIC U-boat wave at a Ju 88C-6 of V./KG 40 as it performs a low flypast over the vessel off the French coast in 1943 (*Author's collection*)

By 1942 the Battle of the Atlantic was being fought further away from the Bay of Biscay, and the Allies quickly realised that U-boats had to transit through this body of water to either get to their hunting grounds or return to their French bases. Destruction of these vessels was left to the aircraft of RAF Coastal Command's No 19 Group, flying from airfields in southwestern Britain.

The only German aircraft available to counter the RAF out over the Bay early on were lightly armed Ar 196 floatplanes of 5./*Seeaufklärungsgruppe* 196. With an offensive armament of two 20 mm cannon and one 7.92 mm machine gun and high manoeuvrability, the Ar 196 did enjoy modest success against Whitleys and, to a lesser extent, Sunderland flying boats, but when matched against heavily armed Beaufighters, the result was very one-sided in RAF Coastal Command's favour. It was obvious to the Luftwaffe that some form of long-range fighter cover was needed. No solution was immediately found.

By early 1942, the latest version of the Ju 88C-6 was coming off the production line. With increased offensive and defensive armament, the fighter was chosen by the Luftwaffe on 23 June 1942 to protect U-boats entering and leaving the Bay of Biscay. Three days later, four Ju 88C-6s fresh from the production line were allocated to the role. They would be based at Bordeaux-Mérignac and operated by *Zerst.St./Küstenfliegergruppe* (Zerst.St./Kü.Fl.Gr.) 106 or Zerst.St./KG 6 (Kü.Fl.Gr. 106 was subordinated to the recently formed *Stab.*/KG 6, prior to it becoming II./KG 6 at the end of August 1942), being subordinate to Fw 200 unit III./KG 40. On 2 July 1942 it was announced that the *Staffel*'s strength would be increased by a further 24 Ju 88C-6s.

Zerst.St./Kü.Fl.Gr. 106 was still in existence on 25 August 1942, but five days earlier, the formation of 13./KG 40 had been announced. It would be formed from Zerst.St./Kü.Fl.Gr. 106, supposedly as part of IV./KG 40. With the arrival of more aircraft, which allowed the formation of 14./KG 40, both *Staffeln* were assigned to newly established V./KG 40 towards the end of August. 15. *Staffel* would be formed on or around 12 September.

It is believed that the first victory for the new unit came on 15 July 1942 when Feldwebel Henny Passier shot down a Wellington of No 311 Sqn flown by Flt Sgt Hugo Dostal, resulting in the deaths of its Czech crew. Passier, who had been posted to KG 40 from the training *Staffel* 10.(*Ergänzungs*)/KG 3, would be killed on 17 September whilst flying with 13./KG 40. A second victory went to Leutnant Karl Stöffler of *Stab* III./KG 40 (he had formerly served with Zerst.St./KG 6) on 20 July when he shot down a Wellington of No 15 OTU and damaged a second bomber, although the latter aircraft in turn shot him down. Two days later, Hauptmann Carlhanns Weymar, who was apparently the *Staffelkapitän* of Zerst.St./KG 6, was killed when his aircraft collided with an Fw 200.

Following just one victory claim for the Ju 88C-6 in August 1942, RAF losses would rise the following month when eight anti-submarine aircraft were lost to V./KG 40, all but two of them being claimed by 13. *Staffel*. Closer to Brittany, 8./JG 2, equipped with Fw 190s at Brest and under the leadership of Oberleutnant Bruno Stolle, had also been tasked with playing its part against the RAF's growing anti-submarine aircraft threat. The *Staffel* also claimed eight RAF aircraft destroyed in September.

The air war now began to escalate in its ferocity. On 20 July, Beaufighters of No 235 Sqn had moved to RAF Chivenor, in Cornwall, and they soon began flying fighter sweeps in support of anti-submarine aircraft. Similarly equipped, No 248 Sqn would arrive at RAF Talbenny, in Wales, in mid-September.

Apart from some successes against the Ar 196s, it was not until 8 September that No 235 Sqn first met V./KG 40, shooting down Leutnant Wolfgang Graf von Hönsbröch of 13./KG 40 shortly after he had downed the Hudson of No 500 Sqn flown by Sgt Sam Pearce – all but one of Pearce's crew were captured, while all three Germans were killed.

The following day, Hauptmann Paul Heide, *Staffelkapitän* of 13./KG 40, was lost

Spotless in appearance, this particular Ju 88C-6 from V./KG 40 is believed to have been flown by the *Geschwaderkommodore*, Major Robert Kowalewski, during the latter half of 1942, but not on operations. Photographs show the aircraft bearing the famous 'World in a Ring' insignia of KG 40, which was not seen on any other V. *Gruppe* Ju 88C-6s (*Author's collection*)

in combat with a Whitley of No 77 Sqn flown by Sgt Bill Hilton (the bomber was also shot down). A further four Ju 88s were downed, mostly by No 235 Sqn, before the month was out as RAF Coastal Command Beaufighter units tried to achieve air superiority over the Bay of Biscay. However, in October, V./KG 40 claimed six RAF aircraft destroyed, including, at last, one of its protagonists from No 235 Sqn when Feldwebel Wilhelm Arians of 14. *Staffel* downed Plt Off Bill Hollis and his navigator, Sgt Henry Taylor, on the 21st. The month's only combat loss in return was Feldwebel Helmut Wagner of 13./KG 40, who fell to No 248 Sqn on 8 October.

November was much quieter, with just two combat losses being suffered on the 1st, again caused by No 235 Sqn. This unit and No 248 Sqn would, in turn, lose four Beaufighters to 8./JG 2 during the course of the month, followed by nine more in December.

Even though there were few combats and operational losses for V./KG 40 in the final weeks of 1942, accidents were more commonplace. One such incident claimed the life of the *Gruppenkommandeur*, Hauptmann Gerhard Korthals, who had flown He 111 pathfinders with 2./*Kampfgruppe* 100 and then Ju 88s with 8./KG 51. Awarded the German Cross in Gold in July 1942 and the Knight's Cross on 21 October, two weeks after receiving the latter decoration he was killed in a freak accident when his Ju 88C-6 crashed during a tactical training flight. It was discovered that a mechanic had lost his cutlery from his overall pocket whilst checking the oil level in one wing. One of the errant implements then got itself stuck in an aileron during the subsequent flight, restricting the controls and causing the aircraft to crash.

As the year drew to a close, the first USAAF aircraft began to appear in the Bay of Biscay. Because of the heavy demands placed on RAF Coastal Command due to the large movement of shipping towards North Africa following Operation *Torch*, Allied air traffic had also increased in the area. V./KG 40 encountered American B-24s a number of times, and on 21 November the USAAF claimed to have shot down three Ju 88C-6s in a running battle between 13. *Staffel* and Maj Ramsay Potts Jr, the Commanding Officer of the 93rd BG's 330th Bombardment Squadron (BS), operating from RAF Holmesley South in Hampshire. The Americans thought that their assailants were Me 210s, but Unteroffizier Heinz Hommel of 13./KG 40 noted the inconclusive combat in his logbook. No German aircraft were lost.

At the same time, the crews of six B-24s of the 409th BS/93rd BG detached to RAF St Eval, in Cornwall, from 22–24 November reported a number of inconclusive combats with the Luftwaffe. Earlier that same month, on the 10th, the 1st Antisubmarine Squadron (ASS) of what was to become the 480th Anti-Submarine Group (ASG) had arrived at RAF St Eval for the remainder of 1942, although it initially had little impact on operations in the Bay of Biscay.

As was the case for much of November, V./KG 40 saw little in the way of action during the first three weeks of December. On the 17th, four aircraft from 14. *Staffel* on a *Freie Jagd* (fighter sweep) intercepted a Whitley, carrying out nine attacks and hitting it in the starboard engine and fuselage. As it then disappeared into cloud, no claim could be made. However, Leutnant Artur Thies should have been credited with its destruction, for a Whitley of No 10 OTU flown by Sgt Maurice Denham failed to return from operations over the Bay of Biscay. The bodies of three of the crew (including Denham) were later washed ashore in Brittany.

With the build-up in North Africa continuing and the volume of Allied air traffic crossing the Bay still high, it was only a matter of time before V./KG 40 intercepted one of the transiting formations. To keep clear of 8./JG 2, the USAAF fighters and bombers flew much further out to sea. This meant that intercepting them would be a matter of luck, and on 23 December, after a very quiet month for the Ju 88C-6 crews, good fortune was with V./KG 40.

On this day, Lt Col Bill Covington led a flight of 51 P-38 Lightnings of the 82nd FG to Gibraltar. For navigation, an A-20B Havoc flown by Capt Don Martz of the 47th BG would lead them. About two hours out from RAF St Eval, the massive formation was bounced by four aircraft from 14./KG 40. In the confusion that followed, Oberfeldwebel Georg Heuer, another pilot posted to V./KG 40 from 10.(*Ergänzungs*)/KG 3, shot down the A-20B – something that was not seen by any of the P-38 pilots, who were concerned with their own survival.

Meanwhile, 14. *Staffel* was credited with shooting down the Lightning flown by Lt Earl Green of the 95th FS, who was reported missing. Lt Arthur Broadhead of the 96th FS turned back and crash-landed on the beach at Clare, in Ireland, while Capt Buddy Strozier, also of the 96th FS, force-landed in Portugal. Finally, Lt Theo Miller of the 97th FS crash-landed in Spain and Lt Frank Henderson of the 96th FS was killed in a crash upon arriving in Algeria. Although the Lightning pilots in turn claimed to have shot down a Ju 88, none were lost.

The onset of bad weather meant V./KG 40 only saw action again on 30 December prior to the new year. On that date the *Gruppe* was credited with shooting down a B-17 returning from an attack on the U-boat pens at Lorient. With III./JG 2 also claiming eight Flying Fortresses, and two more unconfirmed, on that same day, and with only three B-17s lost in total, the identity of the aircraft shot down cannot be determined.

Two hours before this action, 17 P-39 Airacobras of the 16th Observation Sqn/68th Observation Group en route to Oufda, in French Morocco, with a B-25 as their mothership, were bounced by V./KG 40. Oberfeldwebel Georg Heuer shot down Lt Verne Lincoln Jr, who bailed out but was reported missing in action. V./KG 40 in turn lost its *Gruppenkommandeur*, Hauptmann Helmut Dargel, his aircraft being seen in combat with another P-39 350 km southwest of Lorient. He was the second *Gruppenkommandeur* to be killed in just six weeks. Temporary command went to Hauptmann Alfred Hemm, formerly of III./KG 40, who had been handling the administrative duties for Dargel since 13 November. He would take over officially at the start of March 1943, at which point he was promoted to Major.

V./KG 40's first combat for 1943 took place on 3 January when two crewmen from 15. *Staffel* were wounded by return fire from a B-17 that was attacking Lorient. However, for much of the remainder of the month, a series of uneventful searches for U-boats, *Freie Jagd* and reconnaissance missions resulted in no enemy contact. The first conclusive contact with the RAF came on 29 January when four Beaufighters of No 248 Sqn led by Flt Lt Aubrey Inniss shot down two aircraft (flown by Oberfeldwebel

Johannes Kriedel and Unteroffizier Paul Paschoff) from V./KG 40 in a very one-sided combat without suffering any losses themselves.

The engagement the following day was far more spectacular. Again, it involved No 248 Sqn, except this time the Beaufighter crews were outnumbered when they bounced a *Schwarm* from 14./KG 40. The latter aircraft, led by *Staffelkapitän* Hauptmann Hans-William Reicke, were flown by Oberfeldwebel Ernst Mündlein, Oberleutnant Hermann Horstmann and Oberfeldwebel Georg Heuer.

The initial bounce resulted in Heuer's Ju 88C-6 being shot down by Flt Sgt J Duncan, but what happened after that is unclear. Mündlein reported that Reicke had just shot down a Beaufighter when he collided with another RAF fighter that was attacking him, and both aircraft plunged into the sea – this was also observed by Duncan. Horstmann's fighter was damaged at some point and returned on one engine. No 248 Sqn lost Beaufighters flown by Sgt Stuart Bell and Flg Off Elson Cunningham.

The death of 31-year-old Reicke was another serious blow to V./KG 40's senior ranks. The *Gruppe*'s Executive Officer was a very experienced maritime pilot, having flown He 115s with Kü.Fl.Gr. 506, Do 26s with the *Transozeanstaffel*, Do 17s with Kü.Fl.Gr. 606, Fw 200s with I./KG 40 and Ju 88s with Kü.Fl.Gr. 106. He was also a very popular *Staffelkapitän*.

February was again a relatively quiet month for all involved. On the 5th Oberleutnant Hermann Horstmann from 14./KG 40 shot down an Airacobra attempting to reach North Africa via Gibraltar. Five 346th FS/350th FG Airacobras, again being 'navigated' by a lone USAAF bomber, had taken off from an airfield in Cornwall and soon met very thick cloud. Not long after, the small formation became totally lost. Lt Clyde Wilson followed the coast to Spain where, out of fuel, he landed at a Spanish airfield. Lt Charles Kirchner decided to head back to England and ended up landing safely in Northern Ireland. Lt Henry Nelson was shot down and killed by Horstmann.

The next combat took place four days later. Due to predation by Beaufighters, V./KG 40 was now being forced to sortie a minimum of four Ju 88C-6s as a *Schwarm*, thus providing mutual protection. During the afternoon of 9 February, at least two *Schwarm* from 15./KG 40 were engaged in a sea search and *Freie Jagd* when, just before 1500 hrs, four aircraft from one of the *Schwarm* spotted three Beaufighters from No 248 Sqn. These aircraft were being led by Sqn Ldr David Cartridge, a pilot who was destined to become one of RAF Coastal Command's top aces.

The two formations manoeuvred to get into the best position for an attack and then tore into each other. In a very confused dogfight, Leutnant Dieter Meister (another of V./KG 40's future *Experten*) claimed to have shot down two Beaufighters. The aircraft flown by Flt Lt George Melville-Jackson was the only Beaufighter to suffer any damage. No 248 Sqn claimed three Ju 88s in return, and Oberleutnant Franz

Officers of 14./KG 40 pose for a group photograph in the summer of 1942. They are, from left to right, Leutnant Hermann Flothmann (killed on 1 November 1942), Leutnant Herbert Hintze, Leutnant Heinz Olbrecht, *Staffelkapitän* Hauptmann Hans-William Reicke (killed on 30 January 1943), Leutnant Artur Thies (killed on 22 March 1943) and Leutnant Helmut Messerschmidt (killed on 11 April 1944) (*Author's collection*)

Isslinger and Oberfeldwebel Heinrich Dettmer were lost. As usual, there were no survivors from either crew.

Another month would pass before the next victory was achieved when Meister shot down the No 10 OTU Whitley flown by Sgt John Ingram on 10 March. Although only a training unit, it was operating over the Bay of Biscay on anti-submarine patrols with crews destined for RAF Bomber Command that were barely combat ready.

Twelve days later, the first Operation *Instep* kills occurred when No 264 Sqn Mosquitos shot down two 14. *Staffel* fighters, the RAF Fighter Command unit having been detached to RAF Coastal Command to counter the increased German air activity over the Bay. On 23 March, the first RAF Fortress (a Mk IIA) was shot down by Hauptmann Hans Morr, *Staffelkapitän* of 15. *Staffel*. The radio transmission from No 59 Sqn's Flg Off Richard Weatherhead at 1310 hrs stating that he was being attacked matched Morr's signal that he was engaging a Fortress.

About an hour later, an RAF Ferry Command Liberator of No 511 Sqn, which was returning to Britain from Gibraltar carrying, amongst its passengers, the Air Officer Commanding Gibraltar, Air Vice-Marshal Robert Whitham, was shot down by Leutnant Ulrich Hanshen of 15./KG 40. During the latter combat, Leutnant Friedrich Apel misjudged his attack on the relatively defenceless Liberator and dived into the sea.

The following day (24 March) saw no let up in this sudden flurry of activity. Oberleutnant Hermann Horstmann shot down his third confirmed victim in the form of a Halifax of No 58 Sqn, whose gunners killed two of Horstmann's crew in return, forcing him to land at the Spanish airfield of La Albericia.

At that point, Horstmann was unaware that after being with 13./KG 40 for just two months, today would see him being given command of 13. *Staffel*. Whilst on another mission that day searching for U-665, and for reasons that are not clear, Hauptmann Georg Esch, the *Staffelkapitän* of 13./KG 40, crashed into the sea north of the Spanish coast. All three crew were seen to get into a dinghy and a frantic rescue attempt began. In an effort to rescue Esch, it was reported that Leutnant Dieter Meister flew to the Spanish mainland and a crew member bailed out so that he could direct the locals to the dinghy. However, this desperate plan failed, and the bodies of Esch and his crew were later washed ashore and buried at La Coruna.

April 1943 would see an improvement in the weather and an increase in the number of inconclusive actions being fought. Indeed, V./KG 40 recorded just one victory, and suffered no combat losses. The solitary success went to future ace Leutnant Albrecht Bellstedt of 14. *Staffel*. He had completed his first operational flight on 28 February 1943, but it was not until his fifth sortie on 10 April that he finally encountered the RAF.

Seen here sat in the cockpit of a Ju 88C-6, Leutnant Dieter Meister initially served with 13./KG 40 before subsequently becoming *Staffelkapitän* of 3./ZG 1. His tally of ten aircraft shot down over the Bay of Biscay earned him the German Cross in Gold. Meister was killed in action on 21 November 1944 whilst serving as *Staffelkapitän* of Fw 190-equipped 10./JG 2 (*Author's collection*)

Albrecht and another Ju 88 had taken off to escort the Italian blockade breaker *Himalaya*, while Flt Sgt James Hoather, flying a Halifax of No 58 Sqn, had sortied from RAF St Eval to locate the same vessel. The Halifax crew reported being attacked by two Ju 88s, their bomber receiving slight damage, but they in turn claimed to have probably destroyed one of their attackers and damaged the second. Bellstedt reported attacking the Halifax four times and his fighter was hit 11 times, but no German aircraft were lost or badly damaged. Hoather would be awarded the Distinguished Flying Medal for this action on 10 April, only to be shot down and killed by V./KG 40 on 9 May.

Bellstedt added to his tally on 17 April when he shot down the Whitley flown by Sgt Leonard Smith and Flg Off Colin Thwaites from No 10 OTU. There were no survivors from the six-man crew.

May brought a change in U-boat tactics, the *Befehlshaber der U-Boot* (Commander of the U-boats), Konteadmiral Eberhard Godt, writing at the start of the month;

'Enemy air forces have made themselves felt over the approaches to Biscay to a very marked degree – losses and damage in this area have again sharply increased, as during the period before the first improvised radar interception sets were introduced [to U-Boats].

'Anti-aircraft armament is being strengthened as a counter-measure, but the solution can be considered satisfactory only when the boats' armament permits them to remain on the surface to fight it out with the aeroplanes, or at any rate when it is essential for boats attacking a convoy to get ahead to make an attack despite enemy air escorts.'

With an increasing number of Allied aircraft operating over the Bay, the U-boat force was more reliant than ever on V./KG 40's protection. Sadly, the poor level of air combat training offered to the *Gruppe*'s crews meant losses would steadily rise as the RAF sought to dominate the skies.

The first conclusive combat and victory of the month was fought on the 13th when Feldwebel Vincenz Giessübel, a former bomber, nightfighter and intruder pilot from I./NJG 2 who was now flying with 13. *Staffel*, shot down a No 224 Sqn Liberator. Two days later, flying with Leutnant Martin Reuter of 15./KG 40, Giessübel helped shoot down the first Sunderland (from No 228 Sqn) to be claimed by the *Gruppe* in eight months. From

A Ju 88C-6 of 13./KG 40 comes in close for the benefit of a photographer onboard an Fw 200 from KG 40 in 1943. The pilot is having to fly with the nose of his fighter in a raised position in order to stay in formation with the appreciably slower Condor. Note the white band on the spinner of the Ju 88C-6, denoting that the four escorting aircraft are indeed from 13. *Staffel* (*Author's collection*)

then on, V./KG 40 would inflict a heavy toll on units equipped with the flying boat, despite its reputation for being heavily armed. That said, Ju 88C-6s from 15. *Staffel* were also lost whilst in the process of shooting down Sunderlands on 15 and 17 May.

On 7 May, prior to V./KG 40 seeing action that month, a number of crews from 13. *Staffel* had flown to Amsterdam-Schiphol airfield and commenced flying missions over the North Sea. Their transfer north was probably prompted by a Kriegsmarine request for better fighter cover following recent attacks on their coastal convoys by RAF and Fleet Air Arm aircraft. Although no encounters with such machines subsequently transpired, logbooks from crews involved record attacks on British motor torpedo boats and fishing vessels. The only notable mission of the whole detachment occurred on 14 May, when aircraft flew within visual range of Lowestoft. A conspicuous lack of success meant the detached crews had returned to Lorient by 28 May, and they recommenced operations over the Bay the following day.

In response to the sudden flurry of German air activity caused by the change in U-boat tactics, Beaufighters of No 235 Sqn were again detached to Cornwall to assist both No 248 Sqn and the *Instep* Mosquitos. No 235 Sqn's Sqn Ldr Tony Binks, with Flg Off Howard Vandewater, had an immediate impact in-theatre on 20 May when they shot down Leutnant Hans Vieback of 13./KG 40.

The increased operational tempo began to push the various *Staffeln* closer to the 500 missions mark, and it is possible that competition to be the first *Staffel* to achieve this notable milestone could have, at this time, dictated some of the sorties flown. This honour eventually fell to 14. *Staffel* on 21 May, with its *Staffelkapitän*, Leutnant Kurt Necesany flying the mission in question. 13. *Staffel*'s 500th took place on 1 June – a date that saw V./KG 40 credited with downing an aircraft carrying Leslie Howard, one of Britain's most able film actors.

Celebrating 14./KG 40's 500th operational mission, on 21 May 1943, the pilot who flew the sortie in question, *Staffelkapitän* Oberleutnant Kurt Necesany, offers his hand to an unnamed crewman for a congratulatory handshake. In the background is a Ju 88C-6 coded F8+GY (*Author's collection*)

RAF losses began early that day. No 420 Sqn had recently been detached to the Middle East, and the unit had begun ferrying its Wellingtons there via North Africa. In order to be clear of the Bay of Biscay before V./KG 40 was on the prowl, most aircraft had taken off from Portreath, in Cornwall, in darkness. On this day, the first Wellington departed at 0421 hrs, with two more following at short intervals, headed for Ras al Mar, in Morocco.

Unfortunately for No 420 Sqn, at least five Ju 88s of 13./KG 40 led by Oberleutnant Hermann Horstmann had taken off from Lorient at 0656 hrs on an armed reconnaissance. Just over an hour later, they spotted the first of the Wellingtons, flown by Sgt Alexander Sodero. After a short combat, Horstmann was credited with shooting it down. Fifteen minutes later, they attacked a second flown by Flg Off Gordon McCulloch, whose destruction was credited to Unteroffizier Heinz Hommel.

As 13. *Staffel* returned triumphantly from its 500th operational mission, the unit's aircraft were replaced by eight Ju 88C-6s from 14. *Staffel* led by Oberleutnant Herbert Hintze which had taken off from Bordeaux at 1000 hrs to look for, and escort back, two U-boats. Because of poor weather conditions, the search for the vessels was called off and the fighters continued on a general patrol. At 1245 hrs a DC-3 was spotted heading north, and five minutes later 14./KG 40 attacked.

Flight 777-A had taken off from Lisbon, in Portugal, bound for Whitchurch airfield near Bristol at 0735 hrs GMT. The aircraft, a KLM (Royal Dutch Airlines) DC-3 flown by Capt Quirinius Tepas, had a Dutch crew of three and a passenger compliment of eight males, three females, a child and an infant. One of the passengers was the famous Hollywood actor Leslie Howard. As the DC-3 tried to get away, it was attacked and shot down by Leutnante Albrecht Bellstedt and Max Wittmer-Eigenbrot. There were no survivors.

There would be one final loss that day when a Halifax of No 58 Sqn flown by Flt Lt Francis Gilmore was shot down by Hauptmann Heinz Morr, assisted by Leutnant Lothar Wolff, of 15./KG 40. A total of 38 people had lost their lives on 1 June, and no German aircraft had been downed in return.

Ju 88Cs of 14./KG 40 taxi out at either Lorient or Bordeaux-Mérignac, in western France, to signal the start of another mission over the Bay of Biscay in the late summer of 1943. The aircraft closest to the camera was one of the first Ju 88C-6s flown by the *Staffel* to feature the maritime-inspired lighter grey camouflage scheme (*Author's collection*)

The days that followed saw a series of combats and skirmishes in which the RAF always came off worse. The most costly loss during the following two weeks was when, on 3 June, a Hudson of No 1 OADU was shot down by Leutnant Heinz Olbrecht from 14./KG 40. Returning to North Africa in the aircraft were seven passengers, all squadron leaders or above in rank, who were killed. The most senior was Gp Capt Robert Yaxley, who had commanded Beaufighter-equipped Nos 252 and 272 Sqns prior to taking command of No 117 Sqn. He had led No 249 (Transport) Wing since February 1943.

Two other passengers were experienced fighter pilots, both of whom had fought in the Battle of Britain. Wg Cdr Howard 'Billy' Burton had recently finished his tour as Wing Leader of No 239 (Kittyhawk) Wing and was returning to North Africa to a new job following a spell of leave, whilst Sqn Ldr Osgood Hanbury had just completed his tour as the CO of No 260 Sqn and was also returning to North Africa after leave.

11 June saw the second *Instep* kill over the Bay of Biscay. Flt Lt Joe Singleton of No 25 Sqn had been detached, with three other crews, to No 264 Sqn at Predannack, in Cornwall. On what was to be his last *Instep* before rejoining his squadron at RAF Church Fenton, in North Yorkshire, he had led a formation of six aircraft and was credited with shooting down Feldwebel Fritz Hiebsch of 15./KG 40. However, as potent as they were to Ju 88C-6s, the Mosquitos were vulnerable to Fw 190s – on 13 June, Oberfeldwebel Fritz May and Feldwebel Alois Schnöll of 8./JG 2 accounted for two aircraft from No 25 Sqn and one from No 410 Sqn as they returned from an *Instep* patrol.

For the remainder of June, despite high levels of air activity over the Bay, combats between V./KG 40 and the RAF decreased. Only two more Ju 88s were lost, with the aircraft flown by Leutnant Willi Gutermann from 14. *Staffel* on the 19th definitely falling to Mosquitos of No 151 Sqn. It is probable that a second aircraft from 13./KG 40 lost that same day was also the victim of a Mosquito. Gutermann and his crew survived the ditching and, two days later, were picked up by a fishing boat off the Spanish coast. They were repatriated, but did not resume operations until mid-September.

The only operational loss for V./KG 40 in July occurred on the 12th during a combat with a Whitley of No 10 OTU flown by Sgt Charles Rudman. Although the bomber was destroyed by Oberleutnant Hans Schuster, Unteroffizier Georg Frassek's fighter was also shot down. After ditching and clambering into a dinghy, Frassek and his crew were picked up by the Royal Navy. They were the first personnel from V./KG 40 to be captured, and although they were initially very security conscious, over the next few months the RAF managed to piece together a very comprehensive report on the *Gruppe*. It included a unit history, projected expansion, aircraft used, aircraft range and armament, strength and losses, activities, tactics and *Gruppe* personalities.

The document gave a fascinating insight into what was hitherto a mystery Luftwaffe unit. For example, the fact that the *Gruppe* was based at Bordeaux but also operated out of Lorient (and occasionally Cognac) resulted in an air attack on Lorient in September in an attempt to prevent the airfield's use by V./KG 40, and to destroy the aircraft of whichever *Staffel* was based there at the time.

Leutnant Knud Gmelin of 13./KG 40 looks down from the cockpit of his Ju 88C-6, which has the new camouflage scheme favoured for maritime operations by V. *Gruppe* from the summer of 1943. Gmelin joined 13. *Staffel* in April 1943 and he would eventually be killed in action on 9 June 1944 leading 1./ZG 1 over the Normandy beaches following D-Day. Although he was credited with shooting down 13 Allied aircraft over the Bay of Biscay, Gmelin had received no major decorations prior to his death (*Author's collection*)

Despite the RAF now being aware of the *Gruppe*, its aircraft and its operational bases, V./KG 40 still claimed up to nine victories in August. This month would, in fact, turn out to be the busiest and bloodiest in the *Gruppe*'s short life. This was primarily due to the arrival of more USAAF aircraft over the Bay of Biscay – just 15 hours into 1 August, the first to die would be an American.

It was felt that RAF Coastal Command had insufficient aircraft to control all of the Atlantic, and following personal requests, at the end of June 1943, the first elements of the 479th ASG began to arrive in the Britain. By 7 July, the 4th and 19th ASSs were established at RAF St Eval, and on 13 July the first operational mission over the Bay was flown. However, on 25 July, the US Navy, in preparation for taking over the mission from the USAAF, sent PBY-5 Catalina flying boats to operate from of Pembroke Dock in South Wales.

Assigned to VP-63, The Catalinas were equipped with magnetic anomaly detectors to hunt U-boats. On 1 August, the flying boat commanded by Lt Bill Tanner, who had been instrumental in detecting and sinking a Japanese midget submarine off Pearl Harbor on 7 December 1941, became the first American anti-submarine victim of V./KG 40.

German pilots who were known to have participated in this engagement were Leutnant Knud Gmelin and Unteroffizier Heinz Hommel of 13. *Staffel* and Leutnante Friedrich Maeder and Lothar Wolff of 15. *Staffel*. Having intercepted the PBY, the Ju 88C-6 crews carried out a series of coordinated attacks from either side, each pass resulting in the death or wounding of a crew member in the flying boat. The final attack came from head-on, killing the bow gunner and wounding Tanner. He and two crew were eventually rescued after landing in the PBY, but seven crew died.

Gmelin's fighter was damaged during the clash, and just over an hour later he was forced to ditch. The crew successfully boarded their dinghy and were rescued by a Bizerte seaplane flown by *Staffelkapitän* Oberleutnant Erwin Voss of 1. *Seenotstaffel* three hours after ditching. They were flown to Brest, from where, following a medical check-up and a night's rest, they were picked up the next afternoon by Leutnant Lothar Wolff in V./KG 40's Bf 108 and flown back to Lorient. Once home, they were greeted as heroes, having been the first crew from 13. *Staffel* to successfully survive a ditching and having shot down the *Gruppe*'s first (and only) Catalina. The latter was also Gmelin's first kill, albeit a shared one.

For the 479th ASG, missions over the Bay now began to increase, and it was not long before the unit met V./KG 40. On 8 August Capt Reuben Thomas Jr and his crew of nine from the 4th ASS were attacked by eight Ju 88C-6s that carried out a total of 27 passes before, finally, the B-24D plunged into the sea, killing the crew. The victory was credited to Feldwebel Walter Stohl of 14./KG 40.

During August, the US Navy lost four aircraft to V./KG 40, with two more damaged. No fewer than 17 RAF aircraft were also downed by the *Gruppe* that month, with at least two more damaged. One of the losses was of an electronic countermeasures Mosquito flown by Flg Off Edward Salter of No 192 Sqn on 11 August, its destruction being credited to Leutnant Gerhard Blankenberg of 15./KG 40.

German losses were, surprisingly, lighter, all being due to return fire. Aside from Leutnant Knud Gmelin on 1 August, Leutnant Max-Wittmer Eigenbrot of 14. *Staffel* was shot down in combat with a B-24 of the 479th ASG on the 8th (all crew killed), Leutnant Ulrich Hanshen of 15. *Staffel* was shot down on the 23rd (all crew rescued), again in combat with the 479th ASG, and, finally Unteroffizier Ernst Itzigehl also of 15. *Staffel* was downed by either a Liberator of No 311 Sqn or a Sunderland of No 461 Sqn on the 30th (all crew killed).

A B-24D flown by Capt Reuben Thomas Jr of the 479th ASG is about to be shot down off the Spanish coast on 8 August 1943. Note the Ju 88C-6 pulling away in the top left corner of the photograph. Credit for the Liberator's destruction was given to Feldwebel Walter Stohl of 14./KG 40, even though the bomber was attacked by eight aircraft from the *Staffel* (*Author's collection*)

Two notable missions occurred towards the end of August. On the 25th, seven aircraft from 15. *Staffel* took off from Bordeaux just after midday to escort 12 Do 217E-5s of II./KG 100, each Dornier carrying an Hs 293A glide bomb destined for warships of the Royal Navy sailing just off the Spanish coast. The attack was not a success, with only one vessel being badly damaged and a further two lightly damaged. Nevertheless, the following day, 15./KG 40 took off again to locate potential targets and, having found six warships, escorted 14 Do 217s to attack the ships of the 1st Support Group on 27 August. The sloop HMS *Egret* then became the first vessel to be sunk by a glide bomb, while HMCS *Athabascan* was left badly damaged.

The American war against the U-boats and V./KG 40 was now given entirely over by the USAAF to the US Navy's Fleet Air Wing 7, which, in addition to the PB5Ys of VP-63, operated PB4Y-1s – the US Navy designation for its navalised B-24s. The first unit so equipped, VB-103, began operating from RAF St Eval on 30 August, and lost its first aeroplane, flown by Lt Keith Wickstrom, on 2 September.

The new month saw no relaxation from either side, and during the first week alone a series of combats solely with both RAF and US Navy Liberators resulted in the deaths of 29 Allied aircrew and the loss of five bombers. Two Ju 88C-6s and six German aircrew were lost in return.

On 11 September a Mosquito was claimed by Oberfeldwebel Artur Ewert of 14./KG 40. Two Mosquitos of No 307 Sqn returned to RAF Predannack with battle damage, with one of them flown by Sgt Jerzy Brockocki crash-landing. The Polish-manned unit in turn claimed to have shot down three Ju 88s and damaged a fourth. Just one aircraft from 14. *Staffel*, flown by Unteroffizier Franz Huber was lost. Of interest, that morning, No 307 Sqn claimed to have shot down a Bf 110, probably destroyed three more and damaged a further three – II./ZG 1 had recently arrived at Brest, and lost a Bf 110G-2 on the 11th.

The most intriguing combat of the month took place on 18 September and involved a glider. No 295 Sqn had been delivering Horsa gilders to Salé, in Morocco, from mid-August. On this date, a Halifax flown by Flg Off Arthur Norman was towing a glider with British Army pilot Lt John Prout at the controls. Shortly after their escort of four Beaufighters turned back, they were intercepted by up to 12 Ju 88s from V./KG 40, which lined up to carry out coordinated attacks. The Horsa immediately cast off and ditched successfully, leaving the German fighters to concentrate on the Halifax – the latter had just a rear gunner and a wildly swinging tow cable for defence.

Carrying out corkscrewing evasive action, the Halifax made it to cloud, albeit badly damaged, and eventually to Salé. The Horsa crew were rescued by the Royal Navy later in the day and Norman awarded the Distinguished Flying Cross and the rear gunner a Distinguished Flying Medal for their actions.

The remainder of September was an anti-climax, even if, on the 21st, V./KG 40 lost a 13. *Staffel* aircraft to Mosquitos of No 456 Sqn on an *Instep* patrol, while 14. *Staffel* shot down yet another Sunderland, this time from Australian-manned No 10 Sqn.

The battle fought four days later was a rare occasion when neither side emerged as the clear winner. In a confused combat between 12 Ju 88C-6s, five Beaufighters of No 235 Sqn and four Mosquitos of No 307 Sqn, Oberfeldwebel Kurt Gäbler of 15./KG 40 claimed to have shot an aircraft down, although it was credited to Leutnant Martin Reuter also from 15. *Staffel*. The only loss was a Mosquito flown by Flt Sgt Les Lowndes of No 307 Sqn. The Beaufighter flown by Plt Off Len Oakley of No 235 Sqn had its tail shredded by gunfire and crash-landed upon returning to Portreath,

Five Ju 88C-6s of 14./KG 40, all in the maritime grey scheme, fly in close formation in late 1943. F8+RY was normally flown by *Staffelkapitän* Oberleutnant Kurt Necesany during this period, the aircraft being marked with several victory bars on its rudder. The fighter also carried the name *Ruth* on the nose in honour of his fiancée, who was soon to be his wife and then widow (*Author's collection*)

while Flg Off Bernard Hammond was wounded by a cannon shell splinter. V./KG 40 in turn lost single crews from both 14. and 15. *Staffeln*. No 307 Sqn claimed to have shot down seven Ju 88s but this was downgraded to two destroyed, two probably destroyed and three damaged.

All of this came two days after Lorient was bombed and 16 Ju 88C-6s from V./KG 40 were either destroyed or damaged to varying degrees.

With the arrival of autumn, encounters between V/KG 40 and Allied aircraft tailed off dramatically, with only one confirmed victory in October – a Liberator of No 224 Sqn flown by Flt Lt John Rintoul on the 4th, credited to Oberleutnant Kurt Necesany of 14./KG 40 (who was possibly flying with *Stab* V./KG 40 on this date). However, during a series of combats on 7 October with Beaufighters of No 143 Sqn, two Liberators of No 311 Sqn and a B-24 of the 480th ASG, one of the three German pilots lost, which included Oberleutnant Gustav Christner, must have shot down Flt Sgt Ray Cole's Beaufighter (seen to crash into the sea by other members of No 143 Sqn).

German records for that date state two of the three losses were caused by Liberators, while Allied claims were two Ju 88s damaged (No 311 Sqn), one Ju 88 damaged (480th ASG) and two Ju 88s destroyed and one damaged (No 143 Sqn), so it cannot be said for certain who got Cole. A further Ju 88C-6 of 14./KG 40 belly landed at Lorient with a wounded pilot, Unteroffizier Hans Schulzky.

For much of October, an undisclosed number of Ju 88C-6s were detached to Juvincourt and Guyancourt, in northern France. These aircraft were then tasked with shadowing enemy bomber formations attacking Germany in daylight. Although some missions were flown, including on the 14th when the ball bearing factories at Schweinfurt were attacked, no combats resulted. At the end of the month all aircraft returned to duties over the Bay of Biscay.

The detached crews found a changed *Gruppe*, for on 13 October V./KG 40 was re-designated I./ZG 1. The Ju 88C-6s were now reinforced by improved Ju 88R-2s, which began arriving in mid-September 1943. The R-2, powered by BMW 801D engines, had unchanged armament but increased armour and, in particular, an armoured windscreen. The Ju 88s were no longer part of a mixed bomber *Geschwader* (currently consisting, in addition to the Ju 88s, of Fw 200s and He 177s, and having also previously flown Do 217s and He 111s), but were now assigned to a heavy fighter *Geschwader*.

Command of I./ZG 1 was handed to Hauptmann Horst Grahl, formerly the operations officer for V./KG 40, while Oberleutnant Kurt Necesany moved from being *Staffelkapitän* of 2./ZG 1 to become the *Geschwader*'s operations officer. Grahl, posted to V./KG 40 at the end of May 1943, had just the one victory to his name – a Liberator of No 53 Sqn on 8 July, which, in fact, was nursed back to England by Flg Off John Handasyde despite being badly damaged.

Necesany's place as *Staffelkapitän* was taken by Leutnant Albrecht Bellstedt. Hauptmann Hans Morr now formed 7./ZG 1, and in March 1944 this would be expanded to become III./ZG 1, which he would command. The leadership of 3./ZG 1 was given to yet another V./KG 40 veteran, Oberleutnant Hans Schuster.

Aside from promotions and unit commands, recognition of the efforts of the pilots of V./KG 40 in 1943 was also shown in the award of the German Cross in Gold to Leutnant Dieter Meister of 13. *Staffel* and Hauptmann Morr of 15. *Staffel* on 17 October, with Leutnant Bellstedt of 14. *Staffel* receiving the same decoration on 14 November. It had already been given to Oberfeldwebel Ernst Mündlein of 14./KG 40 on 12 July (as a result, no doubt, of his operational service with 2./KG 51 from 1940 until he was posted to V./KG 40 in 1942) and Oberleutnant Hermann Horstmann of 13./KG 40 on 16 August. Oberfeldwebel Kurt Gäbler of 3./ZG 1 would be the final former V./KG 40 pilot to receive this award in March 1944.

November 1943 would prove to be a little more exciting for the 'new' *Gruppe*. The month began with a number of uneventful *Freie Jagd* and escort missions for Fw 200s. Then on the 10th, Leutnant Bellstedt was responsible for the first kill for Ju 88 crews for more than a month when he shot down a Sunderland of No 228 Sqn flown by Flg Off Arthur Franklin. The flying boat was trying to sink U-966, which had been damaged by a Wellington of No 612 Sqn, PB4Y-1s of VB-103 and VB-110 and a Liberator of No 311 Sqn and was now in Spanish territorial waters. The Sunderland crashed and exploded close to the U-boat, and there were no survivors.

The only encounter with RAF fighters that month occurred on 20 November when the new *Staffelkapitän* of 3./ZG 1, Oberleutnant Hans Schuster, was shot down during the course of a fierce dogfight off the Spanish mainland. Crews from Nos 157, 235 and 248 Sqns nevertheless claimed four Ju 88s destroyed and five damaged. I./ZG 1 had been tasked with looking after a Ju 290 of 2./*Fernaufklärungsgruppe* 5 and a Fw 200 of 7./KG 40, but was unable to prevent both aircraft being shot down by Nos 157 Sqn and 248 Sqns, respectively.

A pilot from No 248 Sqn reported seeing a single-tailed twin-engined enemy aeroplane spinning down out of cloud cover and crashing into the sea. This was undoubtedly the last sighting of Schuster, who had probably been separated from the rest of the 3. *Staffel* formation after his aircraft was damaged by a No 157 Sqn Mosquito, only to be ultimately shot down by a No 235 Sqn Beaufighter. Command of 3./ZG 1 now went to Oberleutnant Dieter Meister.

During the last two days of November combats were fought with Australian-manned Sunderlands – one from No 461 Sqn, flown by Flg Off Donald Howe, which was shot down on the 29th, while the flying boat from No 10 Sqn, flown by Flt Lt Clarence Clark, on the 30th managed to return home badly damaged. The crew of the latter aircraft shot down Unteroffizier Hermann Fischer from 2./ZG 1 during the engagement. It was the loss of Fischer that was partly responsible for the series of missions and combats the following day.

On the morning of 1 December, eight Ju 88s that had taken off to search for Fischer were

This Sunderland of No 461 Sqn, flown by Flt Lt Dudley Marrow, was forced down on 16 September 1943. Its destruction was credited to Leutnant Hermann Müller of 14./KG 40 and all of the flying boat's Australian crew were rescued. The aircraft was one of at least 16 Sunderlands claimed by V./KG 40 (*Author's collection*)

bounced by Mosquitos of No 157 Sqn. Leutnant Gerhard Neumann and Obergefreiter Max Vetter of 2. *Staffel* and Unteroffizier Anton Meierl of 3. *Staffel* were shot down. One fighter dived vertically into the sea, the second one ditched, but no survivors were spotted, while Meierl and his crew were seen to clamber aboard a dinghy. The Mosquito flown by Flt Sgt Bill Robertson failed to return, having probably been shot down by Bordfunker Obergefreiter Heinrich Rönsch of 2./ZG 1.

All but one of the surviving Ju 88s returned home, leaving a solitary aircraft circling Meierl's dinghy. It too eventually headed for home, to be replaced by two Ju 88s that found the dinghy being circled by five Beaufighters of No 235 Sqn once they reached it! A short, inconclusive combat ensued before the German aircraft retreated. Meierl's dinghy was spotted by No 157 Sqn later that day and by No 248 Sqn on the 2nd, but he and his crew were never seen alive again.

Another aircraft from 2./ZG 1 had also been lost on 1 December when it was shot down by an American bomber over the Eifel region of Germany while presumably engaged in a shadowing flight. Five Ju 88s had now been lost in just two days, resulting in the deaths of 15 experienced aircrew. Worse was to follow.

For the next 11 days, I./ZG 1 crews were relatively inactive, but with an improvement in the weather on the morning of 12 December six aircraft from 1. *Staffel* took off just after midday to protect reconnaissance aircraft returning from a mission. After less than 30 minutes, one of the Ju 88C-6s suffered an engine failure and Oberleutnant Hermann Horstmann instructed a second aircraft to escort it back to Lorient.

Shortly after 1400 hrs, the surviving four Ju 88s flown by Horstmann, Leutnante Friedrich Maeder and Knud Gmelin and Unteroffizier Franz Frank were confronted by six Beaufighters of No 143 Sqn led by Battle of Britain pilot Wg Cdr Ed McHardy. The only Ju 88 to return was the aircraft of Gmelin, who, with Horstmann, accounted for the Beaufighters flown by Flt Lt Stan Tucker and Flg Off Mike Bentley.

For the final few weeks of 1943, it appears that operations by I./ZG 1 were hampered by poor weather, with only sporadic escort and fighter sweep missions being flown. Further out in the Atlantic, the He 177s of II./KG 40 and Fw 200s of III./KG 40 were actively involved against Allied shipping, albeit with limited success and suffering losses, especially after Christmas Day. The shorter range Ju 88s could do little to influence the final air battles of 1943, or for the ones to come in 1944.

I. and, shortly, III./ZG 1 would exist operationally for just over six months in 1944, and in that time many aircrew would be killed. The new year arrived with a vengeance when, on 5 January, USAAF bombers targeted Bordeaux. Although the vast majority of German fighters defending the city were from JG 2, a number of I./ZG 1's Ju 88s managed to get airborne before the airfield was bombed. Oberfeldwebel Kurt Gäbler of 3./ZG 1 succeeded in shooting down a B-17, presumed to be the aircraft from the 337th BS/96th BG flown by Lt Richard Stakes, which crashed on the eastern edge of Lac d'Hourtin.

Two days later, it was the turn of the recently formed 7. *Staffel*, which was still subordinate to I./ZG 1, both to be blooded and to get its first kill. Whilst on an *Instep* patrol with three other Mosquitos from

No 157 Sqn, Flg Off Philip Huckin spotted two Ju 88s. These were chased until the nearest one was overtaken, attacked and sent crashing into the sea. However, accurate return fire from Feldwebel Johann Pütz's Bordschutze disabled both of the Mosquito's engines and the pilot was forced to ditch 170 miles southwest of Land's End. Huckin and his navigator, Flt Sgt Robert Graham, eventually sailed home thanks to an Airborne Lifeboat that was dropped to them the following day.

Although the remainder of the month was operationally uneventful, a number of crews moved from Bordeaux to Marseille-Istres by both air and bus to start flying escort sorties for anti-shipping operations in the Mediterranean. Even though the move by air went to plan, the journey by road was fraught with danger, for during the night of 16 January the bus was attacked by the French Resistance. The *Kommandeur*, Hauptmann Horst Grahl, who would be awarded the Honour Goblet of the Luftwaffe at the start of February 1944, was slightly wounded. Oberleutnant Herbert Hintze's injuries, however, were far more serious, and he was destined to spend the remainder of the war in a series of hospitals and never flew again.

The first mission over the Mediterranean occurred on 1 February, and Leutnant Robert Baumann, who had moved from 3./ZG 1 to help form the *Gruppe*'s new 7. *Staffel*, participated for what was his 59th operational sortie. The formation was intercepted by Beaufighters of No 39 Sqn, and Flt Sgt Freddie Cooper and Baumann went head to head, shooting each other down (albeit credit was apparently given to Leutnant Ulrich Hanshen of *Stab* III./ZG 1). The two RAF crew and Baumann managed to get into dinghies and were rescued the following day.

Although February saw few combats, on the 14th the PB4Y-1 flown by Lt Ken Wright of VB-103 was shot down by two Ju 88s. The fact that the crash was not observed meant that no claim was filed by the two pilots involved, *Geschwaderkommodore* Oberstleutnant Lothar von Janson and Oberleutnant Kurt Necesany. Two of the US Navy gunners hit one of the Ju 88s, but they too did not see any crash. Von Janson recorded seeing white smoke trailing from Necesany's aircraft, which then ditched and two men were spotted getting into a dinghy.

The following day, I./ZG 1 searched in vain for the experienced Necesany. Apart from damaging a Sunderland of No 10 Sqn flown by Flt Lt John McCulloch, nothing was seen again of the successful 23-year-old Austrian pilot and his crew.

The remainder of February was very much an anti-climax. Apart from occasional fighter sweeps, *Freie Jagd* and uninteresting escort missions for slow Bv 222s of 1./*Seeaufklärungsgruppe* 129, only one further combat occurred when Unteroffizier Fritz Gilfert of 3./ZG 1 shot down a PB4Y-1 flown by Lt Raymond North of VB-105. The aircraft's radio operator managed to send a distress signal stating that they were under attack by enemy aircraft, but a subsequent search of the area only revealed a large oil slick and two dinghies. One of the latter could have also belonged to Feldwebel Heinz

Leutnant Kurt Necesany joined 13./KG 40 in August 1942 and soon proved himself to be a successful fighter pilot. He took command of 14./KG 40 in February 1943, and in October of that same year he moved from being *Staffelkapitän* of 2./ZG 1 to become the *Geschwader*'s operations officer. Necesany was subsequently killed in action attacking a PB4Y-1 of VB-104 on 14 February 1944, by which time he had shot down five aircraft, shared in the destruction of another four and probably destroyed one more (*Author's collection*)

Baldeweg's Ju 88 from 3./ZG 1, which was believed to have been shot down by the PB4Y-1's gunners.

February also saw the continued build up of III./ZG 1. Essentially, the *Gruppe* – commanded by Hauptmann Hans Morr from 7 March 1943, who had handed over 7./ZG 1 to Oberleutnant Martin Reuter formerly of 15./KG 40 – would be employed on the same duties as I./ZG 1 with the exception of one *Staffel*. Its 9. *Staffel* appears to have only existed on paper until May 1944, and 8. *Staffel* did not finish forming until the end of March 1944, and even then it only had limited numbers of aircraft and crews.

Towards the end of 1943, two experimental units were formed under the direct command of *Fliegerführer Atlantik* (Fl.Fü. *Atlantik*). *Sonderkommando Rastedter*, commanded by Hauptmann Siegfried Rastedter, observed, investigated and jammed Allied radio and radar traffic, while the task of *Sonderkommando Kunkel*, commanded by Hauptmann Fritz Kunkel, was to use Ju 88C-6s and Ju 88R-2s equipped with FuG 202 *Lichtenstein* and FuG 227 *Flensburg* airborne intercept (AI) radar against Allied aircraft over the Bay at night. In particular, they were after the RAF's mine-laying aircraft.

Drawing experienced crews from I. and III./ZG 1, such as Leutnant Arthur Ewert of 2./ZG 1 and Oberfeldwebel Kurt Gäbler of 3./ZG 1, the *Kommando* was officially formed on 15 January 1944. However, Kunkel and his crew of Feldwebeln Hans Adam and Alfred Gerber had actually flown the *Kommando*'s first operation – a *Freie Jagd* to Cap Ortegal – on 12 November 1943. By May 1944, the *Kommando* had been re-designated 9.(*Nacht*)/ZG 1 and formed the third *Staffel* within III./ZG 1.

Ju 88C-6 4C+AA of *Sonderkommando Kunkel* in early 1944, this aircraft being fitted with FuG 202 *Lichtenstein* BC, FuG 212 *Lichtenstein* C-1 and FuG 227 *Flensburg* AI radar for nightfighter operations over the Bay of Biscay (*Author's collection*)

The funeral of Hauptmann Erwin Burghoff and his crew from *Kommando Kunkel*, who were killed in a flying accident at Nantes on 21 February 1944, saw three coffins and floral tributes placed in front of an unusually camouflaged Ju 88C-6. Burghoff had previously flown Do 217s whilst serving with *Stab* III./KG 100 (*Author's collection*)

Despite a number of optimistic claims, *Sonderkommando Kunkel* had little to no success, although it did lose crews. On 21 February 1944, Hauptmann Erwin Burghoff, who had recently transferred from *Stab* III./KG 100, and his crew were killed in an accident at Nantes – some records state his unit was *Nachtjagdkommando*/KG 40, but it was in fact *Kommando Kunkel*. The *Staffel* would lose a second aircraft in an accident in April and one was shot down by a Mosquito of the Fighter Interception Unit on 28 June.

March 1944 saw another Mediterranean detachment, with the usual tragic results. During a *Freie Jagd* in and around the Balearic Islands on the 8th, two aircraft from I./ZG 1 (one flown by the popular Oberleutnant Edgar Podzimek) fell victim to Beaufighters of No 153 Sqn, while a third crashed at Saintes-Maries-de-la-Mer west of Marseille. A Beaufighter flown by Flt Sgt Alan Applegate of No 153 Sqn is thought to have been lost to 2./ZG 1 on this date.

The following day saw the scene of battle return to the Bay of Biscay with the arrival of the Imperial Japanese Navy submarine *I 29*. The Germans in turn committed considerable air and surface assets to ensure its safe arrival at Lorient. During the afternoon of 9 March, two Kriegsmarine E-boats and two destroyers set sail to escort the submarine. Meanwhile, ZG 1 had moved to the airfield at Cazaux, towards the south of the Bay, which would allow its aircraft to remain longer on station protecting both the German warships and the Japanese submarine, all of which were now off the north coast of Spain.

This activity did not go unnoticed by the RAF, and on 10 March four Mosquitos from No 248 Sqn, escorting two 57 mm cannon-armed 'Tsetse' Mosquitos from No 248 Sqn's Special Detachment, were sent to attack the submarine and its escorts. The British aircraft found the vessels off Cape Penas being circled by eight Ju 88s. Immediately, the No 248 Sqn Mosquitos tried to draw the German fighters away, allowing the 'Tsetse' aircraft to attack unhindered. Confused dogfights ensued, and

No 248 Sqn claimed to have shot down three Ju 88s and inflicted damaged on the submarine. In reality, only the Ju 88 flown by Feldwebel Karl Bauer of 7./ZG 1 was lost and the submarine sailed on unscathed.

As the Mosquitos withdrew, so did the Ju 88s, only to be replaced by a further formation of aircraft, one of which was flown by the *Geschwaderkommodore* of ZG 1, Oberstleutnant Lothar von Janson. Despite having no operational experience on the Ju 88, von Janson had been given command of ZG 1 on 4 November 1943. However, even by mid-February 1944, Generalleutnant Ulrich Kessler, Fl.Fü. *Atlantik*, said of von Janson, '*Geschwaderkommodore* Oberstleutnant von Janson was not yet fully familiar with this type of aircraft'.

This Ju 88C-6 of *Stab./*ZG 1, photographed in early 1944, is fitted with a single MG 151 cannon and three MG 17 machine guns. The fuselage code <−+− would indicate that the aircraft was either flown by Oberstleutnant Lothar von Janson, who was shot down on 10 March 1944, or by his successor, Oberstleutnant Erich von Selle (*Author's collection*)

The second escort sortie that day was uneventful and, low on fuel, the Ju 88s headed back for Lorient. However, it is believed that the *Kommodore* either became separated or decided to get back to Lorient early. Whatever the reason, it was a fatal mistake. Two sections of two Mosquitos from No 157 Sqn on an *Instep* patrol north and northeast of where No 248 Sqn had carried out its attack earlier that day came across the lone Ju 88. Von Janson took no evasive action until it was too late, and even his gunners did not have time to fire at their attackers. The Ju 88 burst into flames and exploded upon hitting the water. Command of ZG 1 would now pass to Oberstleutnant Erich von Selle, who also had no Ju 88 experience, which probably explains why he appears to have done little operational flying with ZG 1.

For the remainder of the month, missions were flown just over the Bay of Biscay, although now there was an additional new task – an increasing number of sorties closer to the British coast, looking for signs of an Allied invasion fleet. Nevertheless, a *Freie Jagd* on 23 March resulted in the new *Staffelkapitän* of 1./ZG 1, Hauptmann Günther Moltrecht, shooting down a No 461 Sqn Sunderland. The *Staffel* damaged another Sunderland from the same unit eight days later, and on 31 March I./ZG 1 shot down two PB4Y-1s from VB-110. One was credited to Oberleutnant Dieter Meister and the other to the *Gruppe* as a whole.

April was to see the beginning of the end for the Ju 88s of ZG 1. The month started quietly, but the 11th would prove to be a day of carnage brought about by the arrival off Saint-Nazaire of U-255. Two 'Tsetse' Mosquitos of No 248 Sqn's Special Detachment had been tasked with attacking U-255 and its escort vessels. Six more Mosquitos, led by Wg Cdr Oswald Barron, gave close escort to the 'Tsetses', whilst top cover was provided by four Mosquitos from No 151 Sqn led by Wg Cdr Geoff Goodman.

The RAF formation spotted its intended quarry, and at 0935 hrs attacked. Unusually, 1./ZG 1 was in an ideal position to bounce No 248 Sqn, shooting down Wg Cdr Barron and Flt Lt Ken Liversidge. However, the Ju 88 crews failed to see No 151 Sqn above them. The resulting German losses are hard to assess, for there was a second series of combats fought later that day. Nevertheless, No 151 Sqn claimed two destroyed, one probable and one damaged, whilst No 248 Sqn claimed one destroyed and one probable.

Flg Off Keith Kemp and his navigator Flt Sgt Jim Maidment of No 151 Sqn were in turn shot down, with fellow Mosquito crews stating that they had heard a radio call from them stating that they were ditching. Four Mosquitos from the unit duly took off again later that afternoon to try and find the downed crew. Sadly, they were never located. However, No 151 Sqn did encounter Ju 88s from I./ZG 1 also looking for crews shot down that morning. A further three aircraft were claimed destroyed and two damaged in this combat.

Although 1./ZG 1 was in turn credited with the destruction of four Mosquitos, only the aircraft flown by WO Bill Penman failed to return. Flt Sgt Jack Playford's Mosquito was written off upon its return to Predannack due to accurate fire from a Bordschütze in one of the Ju 88s. 1./ZG 1 had lost a total of seven aircraft, with at least two more damaged, in just one day. The cost in human terms was 15 killed, including yet another *Staffelkapitän* (Hauptmann Günther Moltrecht), and five wounded.

On 20 April, four more crews – one from 3. *Staffel* and three from 7. *Staffel*, including that of *Staffelkapitän* Oberleutnant Martin Reuter – were shot down during another escort sortie over the Mediterranean. From then until 6 June, priorities and missions changed. Detachments to Salon to fly missions over the Mediterranean became more permanent. A number of sorties were flown from there, predominantly *Freie Jagd*, and although a mixture of Allied aircraft were encountered, such as Marauders and Lightnings, only one loss occurred, during an escort sortie on 11 May when Unteroffizier Heinrich Lang and his crew from 8./ZG 1 were shot down.

However, it was obvious that an invasion was imminent in northern France. As a result, X *Fliegerkorps* (formerly Fl.Fü. *Atlantik*) tasked ZG 1 to undertake reconnaissance missions looking for signs of the invasion fleet. At the same time, crews began practising low-level flying in preparation for attacks on both Allied shipping and ground targets using cannon and bombs. The invasion commenced on 6 June 1944, and it came as no surprise to the aircrew of ZG 1 when, later that same day, they were thrown into action.

Pitted against superior single-engined Allied fighters and numerous mobile anti-aircraft guns, I. and III./ZG 1 were slaughtered. Oberleutnant Albrecht Bellstedt, *Staffelkapitän* of 2./ZG 1, flew his fourth and final mission over Normandy on 10 June, by which point, 33 aircrew had been killed, three captured and five wounded in just four days.

The precise number of aircraft lost is hard to assess, but suffice it to say that at the start of June 1944, I./ZG 1 had an establishment of 17 Ju 88C-6s, three Ju 88G-1s and ten Ju 88R-2s. By early July, the numbers stood at 13, six and four, respectively. As for III./ZG 1, it had 23 Ju 88C-6s in June and just 11 by July. Among those who were killed between 6–10 June were Oberleutnant Ulrich Hanshen (*Gruppenadjutant* of III./ZG 1) and Leutnante Kurt Löw (*Staffelkapitän* of 7./ZG 1) and Knud Gmelin (*Staffelkapitän* of 1./ZG 1).

Withdrawn from the Normandy front on 10 June, I./ZG 1 operated from Cazaux for the remainder of the month. Oberleutnant Albrecht

Bellstedt then recorded flying seven anti-resistance missions in southern France, his last flight, on 30 June, being his 116th of the war.

On 5 August, I. and III./ZG 1 were disbanded and aircrews sent to other units. I. *Gruppe* would become II./JG 4, while III. *Gruppe* was redesignated III./JG 4 – 9.(*Nacht*)/ZG 1 had already become 1./NJG 4 on 10 July. Mindful that many pilots had only flown the Ju 88 in combat, and some of them the Fw 200 before that, it was criminal that most of them were now retrained as single-seat fighter pilots. For example, Oberleutnant Albrecht Bellstedt was posted to Königsberg to convert to the Fw 190, and on 17 September he became 9./JG 2's *Staffelkapitän*. It is believed he completed just two missions before being shot down and killed in combat, possibly by the P-47-equipped 365th FS/368th FG on 21 October, his Fw 190A-8 crashing in the Limburg–Montabaur area.

After a short period on the staff of the *General der Jagdflieger*, Hauptmann Hans Morr took command of III./JG 76 on 25 August following the death of Hauptmann Egon Albrecht, who had commanded Bf 110-equipped II./ZG 1 in Bay of Biscay operations from late 1943 prior to it becoming III./JG 76. This then became IV./JG 53 around 25 October, and Morr was killed in action four days later flying a Bf 109G. Earlier that month he had been credited with shooting down P-47s on the 3rd and the 15th.

Included in the ranks of the former Ju 88C pilots killed during the final months of 1944 was Oberleutnant Dieter Meister, who perished while serving as *Staffelkapitän* of 10./JG 2 on 21 November after having been retrained to fly the Fw 190. Hauptmann Heinz Schocker, formerly *Staffelkapitän* of 8./ZG 1, was killed on 11 September while leading Bf 109G-equipped 11./JG 4. Finally, German Cross in Gold recipient Oberfeldwebel Ernst Mündlein, who had flown operationally with 2./KG 51 from 1940 until he transferred to V./KG 40, shot down a B-17 on 11 September with 9./JG 4 but was then killed shortly thereafter when his Bf 109G-6 crashed near Bärenstein.

One of the lucky ones to escape the wholesale slaughter of former Ju 88 pilots was *Gruppenkommandeur* Hauptmann Horst Grahl. Promoted to Major on 1 July 1944, and now aged 33, Grahl undertook a series of staff appointments until ending up with *Fliegerführer Kroatien*, working for his old *Kommodore* from his *Stukageschwader* days, Generalmajor Walter Hagen. Another who survived was Oberleutnant Lothar Wolff, who joined 15./KG 40 on 19 May 1943 and was wounded in combat with a Liberator flown by Flg Off John Handasyde of No 53 Sqn on 8 July that same year. He then became *Gruppendjutant* of II.(*Sturm*)/JG 4 on 15 June 1944 and, finally, *Staffelkapitän* of 15./JG 4 on 15 October. Wolff would be credited with single victories while serving with 15./KG 40 and I./ZG 1 and three kills with 15./JG 4.

Oberleutnant Albrecht Bellstedt, *Staffelkapitän* of 2./ZG 1 and Hauptmann Horst Grahl, *Gruppenkommandeur* of I./ZG 1, are seen here in conversation with an unidentified officer. Note that Bellstedt's German Cross in Gold, awarded to him in November 1943, is clearly visible attached to the right breast pocket of his tunic (*Author's collection*)

CHAPTER SEVEN

NIGHTFIGHTING

Ju 88C-4 R4+MT of 9./NJG 2 after suffering what appears to have been engine failure during a sortie from Melsbroek in the late summer of 1942. The aircraft, which lacks AI radar, has yellow spinners to denote its assignment to 9. *Staffel* (*Author's collection*)

To support the Bf 110s, Do 17Zs and Do 215s in the nightfighter role, construction of a newer type of Ju 88C commenced in November 1941, this aircraft being designated the C-6. Ju 88C-2s and C-4s were also used for nightfighting (as well as intruding), but it was the C-6 that carried out the bulk of night operations, as well as operating in other daylight roles as previously detailed in this book.

Ju 88C-6s were assembled at Junkers Flugzeug-und Motorenwerke AG, Zweigwerk Bernburg (JFM-FZB), with components such as wings, fuselages and engines being manufactured elsewhere. Despite assembly starting in November 1941, very few were delivered until the following year, NJG 2 being the initial recipient.

JFM-FZB produced around 99 between November 1941 and May 1942, 149 between June and December 1942 and 209 between December 1942 and April 1943. The vast majority of the C-6s were assembled by Siebel at Halle between April and December 1943 – a maximum of 797. Of course, only a fraction of these airframes were used as nightfighters. Furthermore, from late 1943, a number were converted into Ju 88R-1s or R-2s – essentially Ju 88Cs fitted with BMW 801 engines.

North Africa-based I./NJG 2 recorded its first loss of a Ju 88C-6 on 28 May 1942 when Oberfeldwebel Anton Naiss of 1. *Staffel* was shot down by anti-aircraft guns near Bardia, in Libya. At the start of August, the *Gruppe* was recalled to Melsbroek in preparation for operations over northern France, Belgium and the Netherlands.

Between 4 May and 31 July 1942, I./NJG 2 had claimed 28 Allied aircraft at night in the Mediterranean, but whether the successful pilots were flying C-4s or C-6s cannot be said for certain. However, between 28 May and 2 August 1942, the *Gruppe* definitely lost seven Ju 88C-6s, and following its return to operations from Melsbroek, I./NJG 2's losses were entirely Ju 88C-6s until the superior Ju 88G-1 was introduced.

The Ju 88C-6 would be the first variant to be fitted with AI radar on a regular basis. This was initially FuG 202 *Lichtenstein* BC and then FuG 212 *Lichtenstein* C-1 and FuG 220 *Lichtenstein* SN 2. The Ju 88C-6 was also fitted with the FuG 101 radio altimeter and FuG 227 *Flensburg* radar homer. This equipment, coupled with increased armament and improved range and engines, made the Ju 88C the most potent nightfighter variant to date. It would not be replaced by the Ju 88G-1 until 1944.

While I./NJG 2 was operating in the Mediterranean, II./NJG 2 was formed in November 1941 under the command of Hauptmann Helmut Lent, although it would be equipped with the Do 215 and Bf 110. When II./NJG 2 became IV./NJG 1 in October 1942, and continued to fly the Bf 110, a new II./NJG 2 was formed from III./NJG 2. III. *Gruppe* had flown the Ju 88C following its formation at Gilze-Rijen in March 1942 under the command of Hauptmann Herbert Bönsch, formerly *Staffelkapitän* of Z.St./KG 30 and 1./NJG 2.

A new III./NJG 2 would not emerge until August 1943, when V./NJG 6, formed in June 1943 and commanded by Major Paul Semrau (previously the *Staffelkapitän* of 3./NJG 2), became III. *Gruppe*. It continued to fly the Ju 88C-6.

Hauptmann Herbert Bönsch was destined to play a major part in the early history of III./NJG 2. Although the *Gruppe*'s first victory went to Leutnant Hans-Hermann Müller of 7./NJG 2 (a Boston of No 418 Sqn flown by Plt Off James Willis) on 13 April 1942, Bönsch would claim a Wellington 15 days later (probably from either No 27 OTU or No 300 Sqn). On 10 May, his Ju 88C-2 suffered engine failure during a patrol and he and Gefreiter Georg Sievert were injured in the subsequent force-landing.

On 17 June, Bönsch claimed a Halifax, followed by a Boston nine days later. The latter was, in fact, probably the Hurricane flown by Flt Sgt Gerald Scott of No 1 Sqn. On 24 July, Bönsch claimed a Stirling flown by Flg Off Jack Peel of No 214 Sqn, but a week later he became the first combat loss suffered by III./NJG 2 and his aircraft the first Ju 88C-6 to be downed on nightfighter operations over northern Europe.

Hauptmann Herbert Bönsch (foreground) was formerly *Staffelkapitän* of Z.St./KG 30, and he is seen here wearing the Narvik badge on the left sleeve of his tunic signifying he had flown in Norway in May–June 1940. He took command of 4./NJG 1 upon its formation in August 1940, and remained *Staffelkapitän* after it became 1./NJG 2 the following month. Bönsch eventually moved to *Stab.*/NJG 2 in November 1941, and he was killed in action whilst leading III./NJG 2 on 31 July 1942 (*Author's collection*)

On the night of 31 July, RAF Bomber Command's main target was Düsseldorf. One aircraft taking part in the operation was the No 76 Sqn Halifax flown by Plt Off Walter Waite, who later reported;

'When the aircraft was over Oudorp at about 0130hrs, the Rear Gunner reported an Me 110 [sic] at 1,000yds on the port quarter and immediately after the Mid-Upper Gunner reported another aircraft on the starboard quarter. Unfortunately the Mid-Upper Gunner [Sgt John McAuley] was killed in the ensuing combat, and no other details can be gathered of the action of the second enemy aircraft which was not seen by any other member of the crew. It would appear from the damage done to our aircraft that the enemy aircraft was definitely firing from the starboard quarter and level.

'The enemy aircraft sighted by the Rear Gunner attacked from the port quarter and closed in before opening fire. The Rear Gunner opened fire first at 250yds in two bursts of five seconds. The Mid-Upper Gunner fired a burst of about three seconds at the same time, and was then hit himself and stopped firing.

'The enemy aircraft was firing cannon and machine gun [rounds] into the wings. The enemy seemed to misjudge the relative speeds, having ceased firing and closed into point blank range. The Rear Gunner fired for about ten seconds, with the belly of the aircraft filling his sights and bullets were seen hitting the enemy aircraft. The enemy aircraft pulled straight up and almost immediately dived past the bomber in a steep vertical dive.'

Rear gunner Plt Off Sam Glasgow only claimed the nightfighter as damaged. The damage inflicted to the Halifax was so severe that the crew bailed out after crossing the East Anglia coast, with the bomber crashing near Stock, in Essex. It is possible that Glasgow had shot down Bönsch's Ju 88C-6, which crashed near the Dutch village of Poortugaal at 0125 hrs, killing him, Bordfunker Feldwebel Fw Otto Böttcher and Bordmechaniker Oberfeldwebel August Wille.

Oberleutnant Paul Zorner of 8./NJG 8 gave the following account of the crash site;

'After an hour, a report came from a Flak position that a search party had found the impact site of Bönsch's Ju 88. The plane fell almost vertically onto the road on the edge of the village of Poortugaal, south of Rotterdam, from a height of around 3500m and tore a deep funnel hole into the ground. Only fragments of the crew were recovered from the smashed wreckage.'

Ironically, the night of Bönsch's death had been the most successful so far for III./NJG 2, with a single claim by Hauptmann Walter Fenske of 9. *Staffel*, two by Hauptmann Dr Horst Patuschka, *Staffelkapitän* of 8. *Staffel*, and three for Oberleutnant Heinrich *Prinz* zu Sayn-Wittgenstein, *Staffelkapitän* of 9 *Staffel*. All three were, or would be, aces, and none of them would survive the war.

Fenske was a pre-war pilot who had flown Bf 110s with 2.(Z)/LG 1 and then 14.(Z)./LG 1 before converting to

Aces High! Major Heinrich *Prinz* zu Sayn-Wittgenstein (left), *Staffelkapitän* of 9./NJG 2, is seen here with Hauptmann Paul Semrau, *Staffelkapitän* of 3./NJG 2. Between them, they claimed 129 nightfighter victories – mostly while flying Ju 88s. Note the Narvik badge on the sleeve of Semrau's tunic (*Author's collection*)

Bf 110 nightfighters with 3./NJG 3 in the summer of 1940. Having shot down his first aircraft at night on 24 October 1940, Fenske would join III./NJG 2 in October 1941. Horst Patuschka had no combat experience prior to joining III./NJG 2, as he had been an instructor for most of the war up to then, apart from leading Ju 52/3m-equipped 2. *Kampfgruppe zur besonderen Verwendung* 104 in Norway in April–May 1940. Patuschka would get his first victory with *Ergänzungsgruppe*/NJG 2 on 13 April 1942.

Sayn-Wittgenstein's three victories took his growing tally to 17. A former Beobachter with *Stab* III./KG 1, he had retrained to be a pilot in late 1940/early 1941 and then returned to III./KG 1 for the *Blitz* and Operation *Barbarossa*. In late 1941/early 1942 he was posted to *Ergänzungsgruppe*/NJG 2, with whom he first flew the Ju 88C operationally. Sayn-Wittgenstein's first victory came on 7 May 1942 whilst he was still training on the Ju 88C, and by the time he had joined 9./NJG 2 two months later, he had already taken his total to nine. In the wake of Bönsch's death, Sayn-Wittgenstein took temporary command of III./NJG 2. By the time he had left 9./NJG 2, his score stood at 22, all with the Ju 88C over northwest Europe. He would subsequently increase his tally flying Bf 110s with a number of units on both the Eastern and Western Fronts before returning to command NJG 2 in 1944.

Meanwhile, in the Mediterranean, between February and July 1943, 2. and 3. *Staffeln* initially operated from the Sicilian airfields of Castelvetrano and Comiso, joining elements of the newly reformed II./NJG 2 (Hauptmann Helmut Lent having formed IV./NJG 1 from II./NJG 2 in October 1942). II. *Gruppe* had begun flying from Comiso in late

The *Staffelkapitän* of 9./NJG 2, Oberleutnant Heinrich *Prinz* zu Sayn-Wittgenstein (left), stands by the rudder of his Ju 88C-6 R4+ET at Gilze-Rijen in the autumn of 1942 for a photograph with his crew. The fin of the aircraft is marked with Sayn-Wittgenstein's 21 victories scored to that point, the last being a Liberator – it was probably a Stirling of No 218 Sqn, shot down over the North Sea off Schouwen, in the Netherlands, on 10 September 1942 (*EN Archive*)

November 1942, commanded initially by Hauptmann Dr Horst Patuschka, who now led 4. *Staffel*. Oberleutnant Albert Schulz's 1. *Staffel* had gone on to form 5./NJG 2 and a new 1./NJG 2 was created in February 1943, commanded by Oberleutnant Gerhard Böhme. It would then join 2. and 3./NJG 2 in the Mediterranean.

In addition to the occasional intruder mission and nightfighter sorties, I. *Gruppe* was apparently also tasked with attacking torpedo boats – a secondary and minor role that generated no tangible results, and was not mentioned in surviving logbooks. In fact, I./NJG 2's overall success when performing any of these tasks appears to have been limited. For example, only a handful of enemy aircraft were shot down during its five months in the Mediterranean. The first was credited to Oberleutnant Heinz Rökker, whose victim was probably a Wellington of No 221 Sqn – it lost two aircraft, flown by Sqn Ldr Michael Foulis and Flt Lt Robert Fraser, in the early hours of 19 April 1943. Rökker later reported;

'I received my take off order from Castelvetrano for Raum Mars, near Marsala. At approximately 0100hrs on 19 April, my controller, Oberleutnant Georg Knierim, guided me towards an aircraft, and after 15 minutes I recognised a Wellington flying above me at an altitude of approximately 500m. I attacked it at once from astern, and after firing a burst the left engine was on fire and the aircraft crashed into the sea.'

Two hours after Rökker's claim, Unteroffizier Helmut Ternieden of 3./NJG 2 also reported downing a Wellington (possibly the second No 221 Sqn aircraft, although a Blenheim of No 13 Sqn was also lost that night and a second aircraft damaged, both being engaged by Ju 88s). Finally, Feldwebel Fritz Hobisch of 4./NJG 2 claimed two Whitleys that same night. Strangely, the No 221 Sqn ORB fails to mention the loss of two aircraft on 19 April.

Unteroffizier Hans Kurz of 1. *Staffel* claimed another Wellington (flown by Flt Lt Henrik Van Den Linden of No 162 Sqn) on 19 May. Three days later, the last victory of the detachment again took the form of a Wellington (from No 150 Sqn, the aircraft being flown by Sgt Arthur Williams), the bomber being credited to 1. *Staffel*'s Leutnant Ernst Gross.

Surviving logbooks give some indication of what crews were doing in-theatre. For example, Feldwebel Vincenz Giessübel of 2./NJG 2 arrived at Comiso with a brand-new Ju 88C-6 on 25 February and undertook just 13 operational flights before returning to Germany at the end of July. All but two of these were night patrols in areas named Raum Mars, Raum Neptun, Raum Pollux, Raum Jupiter and Raum Castor. On 11 July, Giessübel flew from Crotone to drop bombs on Syracuse following the Allied invasion of Sicily. The sole daylight mission was a weather reconnaissance on 27 February.

Unteroffizier Erich Hess, Bordmechaniker to Oberfeldwebel Robert Lüddeke of 3./NJG 2, reached Comiso on 6 February. He then flew 15 nightfighter sorties without any success between 16 February and 12 May, as well as one convoy escort and an escort mission for a transport aircraft. On 21 May, Hess, together with the other two members of his crew, were injured in an accident flying to Germany to collect a new aircraft when the Ju 52/3m in which they were travelling crashed at Vibo Valentia, in Italy.

In addition to a number of operational accidents, I. *Gruppe* lost two aircraft in combat during this time. The first was the Ju 88C of Oberleutnant Gerhard Pajung from 2./NJG 2, his aircraft being shot down by Sqn Ldr George 'Pop' Coleman and Sgt L Lyne-Hale of Beaufighter-equipped No 272 Sqn off Cap Bon on 17 April while escorting a convoy. The unit's ORB recorded;

'At 1155hrs, one large motor vessel course believed north on the horizon in a position 37.23N 10.57E. Three minutes later, when at deck level and one mile off Cap Bon, our machine sighted six Ju 88s at deck level, course southwest, and two Ju 88s or Me 110s also at deck level, course northeast. Sqn Ldr Coleman made a quarter stern attack on one Ju 88 travelling southwest, finally finishing close in astern. The engines of the Ju 88 caught fire and the whole aircraft lurched badly, lost height and left formation. A few minutes later, a column of smoke and flames was seen a short distance inland in the direction in which this aircraft had flown. It is claimed as destroyed. Accurate return fire was experienced and Sqn Ldr Coleman's machine was hit in several places and is Cat 1.

'Fg Off Rod Phipps singled out the Ju 88 on the starboard side of the formation and made a beam attack, closing to 200yds astern and seeing strikes all along the fuselage. The starboard engine then caught fire. Fg Off Phipps broke off the attack to have a quick squirt at another Ju 88 but saw no results. The first Ju 88 is claimed as probably destroyed. Aircraft T was not hit.'

The final loss was Oberleutnant Max Castaldo of 3./NJG 2, who failed to return from a mission off Sicily on 21 April. On the 28th, his *Staffelkapitän*, now-Hauptmann Albert Schulz, wrote that the Castaldo crew had taken off at 0300 hrs and, one hour later, they were involved in combat with an enemy aircraft. The last message from them came at 0408 hrs, and at the same time a Flak position on the coast reported an aircraft crashing in flames into the sea. It is believed the Ju 88C was shot down at 0350 hrs off Marsala by Flg Off Reg Foster and Plt Off Maurice Newton of Beaufighter-equipped No 108 Sqn. The crew wrote the following terse report;

'Contact over Marsala, visual on Ju 88 at 1,000ft range, height 12,000ft, ten degrees above dead ahead. Closed to 100yds dead astern and fired one-second burst. Brilliant flash from fuselage and starboard engine. Enemy aircraft dived steeply burning fiercely.'

Feldwebel Giessübel of 2./NJG 2 reported leaving the theatre on 24 July, while Oberleutnant Heinz Rökker had left on 9 June and Oberfeldwebel Hermann Sommer headed for Naples on 31 July. I./NJG 2's second spell in the Mediterranean was finally over, and it would not return again.

II./NJG 2, made up of *Stab*, 4. and 5. *Staffel*, remained in-theatre a little longer, however, operating from Comiso. Reporting just 14 aircraft on strength on 10 July, it too returned north towards the end of the month.

II. *Gruppe* had been more successful than I./NJG 2 in the Mediterranean, claiming 13 aircraft. Officially, the first of these came on 18 January, when Unteroffizier Paul Tolksdorf of 5./NJG 2 badly damaged the Wellington of No 142 Sqn flown by Sqn Ldr James Booth, which was written off after

The identity of who claimed the 20 victory bars that adorn the tail of this Ju 88C-6 from NJG 2 remains unsolved. Hauptmann Heinrich *Prinz* zu Sayn-Wittgenstein shot down his 19th, 20th and 21st aircraft with 9./NJG 2 on the night on 10 September 1942, while Oberfeldwebel Wilhelm Beier, originally with 3./NJG 2, claimed his 20th victory with 7./NJG 2 on 29 July 1942 (*Author's collection*)

landing at Blida, in Algeria. It is possible that the first success actually occurred on the night of 6 January, when Feldwebel Werner Heyne of 5./NJG 2 possibly shot down the No 104 Sqn Wellington of Sqn Ldr Ian Strutt. Heyne failed to return from this mission.

II./NJG 2's final victory in this theatre came on 11 July, when Oberleutnant Walter Riedelberger, also of 5./NJG 2, claimed a DC-3 (either a USAAF C-47 or an RAF Dakota), despite none being reported lost – a number were destroyed the previous night.

During the *Gruppe*'s time in the Mediterranean, its *Kommandeur*, Hauptmann Dr Horst Patuschka, was killed in a flying accident caused by engine failure at Bizerte on 7 March – having by then shot down 23 aircraft, he would be posthumously awarded the Knight's Cross two months later. Although only eight aircraft were lost in action, some 38 aircrew were either killed or posted as missing and a further nine wounded or injured.

In respect to the losses in combat, only two aircraft can be matched with RAF claims. The first was on 28 January, when an aircraft from 5./NJG 2 force-landed with one of its crew wounded at Comiso after having been damaged in combat. Sqn Ldr Jack Urwin-Mann of Spitfire-equipped No 126 Sqn claimed what he thought was an Me 210 over Comiso just before dawn on that date.

The second confirmed loss was on 26 April when a Ju 88C-6 of 4./NJG 2 flown by Unteroffizier Rudolf Nadolny was reported to have been shot down by a nightfighter over Tunisia. The only possible claim was by Sqn Ldr Des Hughes and Flg Off Lawrie Dixon of Beaufighter-equipped No 600 Sqn, who claimed a Ju 88 that crashed in the middle of a field and exploded 35 miles east of Tunis. A number of the aircraft lost

This Ju 88C-6 of II./NJG 2, seen being refuelled in the summer of 1943, is fitted with FuG 212 *Lichtenstein* C-1 AI radar and flame dampers (*Author's collection*)

were referred to in Luftwaffe records as being Ju 88C-6/Lis, indicating that they were fitted with FuG 202 *Lichtenstein* BC radar.

Back in northern Europe, the battle against RAF Bomber Command continued to increase in its intensity. Unlike NJG 2, most German nightfighter units flew a mix of aircraft, so without logbooks, it is hard to be certain that when a successful combat took place, the pilot involved was indeed flying a Ju 88C. For example, NJG 3 was initially a Bf 110 unit commanded by Major Johann Schalk, formerly from III./ZG 26. Only II./NJG 3 began to convert to the Ju 88C in July 1943 at around the time that Major Heinrich *Prinz* zu Sayn-Wittgenstein took command of the *Gruppe*.

To add to the confusion, IV./NJG 3 was formed in November 1942 from parts of III./NJG 2. It was led by Hauptmann Erich Simon, the former *Staffelkäpitan* of 8./NJG 2 who had taken command of III./NJG 2 following the death of Hauptmann Herbert Bönsch. Simon would be killed in action on the night of 7 October 1943 flying a Ju 88C-6. His replacement was experienced Ju 88C pilot Hauptmann Albert Schulz, who had flown intruder missions with 2./NJG 2 and then served as a nightfighter pilot with 1., 3. and 5./NJG 2.

On the Eastern Front, the night bombing war carried out by the Soviet Union was nowhere near as intense as the campaign undertaken by RAF Bomber Command. Short-lived *Nachtjagdschwarm*, which even included He 111s, were at last replaced in August 1943 by NJG 100, initially commanded by Major Heinrich *Prinz* zu Sayn-Wittgenstein. It was the only unit in this theatre to fly the Ju 88C-6 in significant numbers. For example, on formation from IV./NJG 5, which flew a mix of types, it reported 15 Ju 88C-6s with I. *Gruppe*. 4./NJG 100 was formed from 8./NJG 200 in December 1943 (II./NJG 100 did not reach full *Gruppe*

8./NJG 2's Oberleutnant Friedrich Tober suffered an accident at Erfurt-Bindersleben on 24 March 1944 in this Ju 88C-6 equipped with FuG 220. Note the gun barrels of the *Schräge Musik* obliquely-firing 20 mm MG 151 cannon pointing up from the fuselage behind the cockpit of the badly damaged aircraft (*Author's collection*)

status until July 1944), reporting that it had a single Ju 88C-4 and 21 Ju 88C-6s on its establishment.

Although the Ju 88C-6 was nearing the end of its operational life in early 1944, the aircraft continued to soldier on in ever dwindling numbers as best it could until the end of the war. The Ju 88R series had now emerged as its replacement, the R-1 essentially being a C-4 with BMW 801ML engines and FuG 212. The R-2 was identical to the C-6, but again fitted with BMW 801TP engines and FuG 212, FuG 220 or SN 2 radar. The R-1 was built as a conversion of the C-4, while 188 R-2s were constructed from scratch between 1943 and June 1944.

Despite its obsolescence as a nightfighter by late 1943, the Ju 88C-6 was still capable of inflicting telling losses on the enemy when flown to its strengths. The aircraft's most effective exponent, by some margin, in this role was Major Heinrich *Prinz* zu Sayn-Wittgenstein. In mid-August 1943, he had taken command of II./NJG 3 from Major Günther Radusch, and then at the start of December he became *Gruppenkommandeur* of II./NJG 2, replacing Major Herbert Sewing. The latter, a long serving Ju 88C-6 nightfighter pilot, had one victory to his name compared with Sayn-Wittgenstein's 68.

At the start of January 1944, he took command of NJG 2 from the long-serving Oberstleutnant Karl Hülshoff, Sayn-Wittgenstein's arrival coinciding with the intensified nocturnal attacks on Berlin.

Clearly getting the most out of his aircraft, having flown the Ju 88, initially as a bomber, from late 1940, Sayn-Wittgenstein was prolific with his success during the first three weeks of 1944. He shot down six bombers in the early hours of the 2nd, taking his score to 74, one on the 14th, three on the 20th and, finally, on 21 January, four more to take his score to 83. However, after shooting down what would be his final victim, believed to be a Lancaster flown by Flt Lt Leslie Kilvington of No 156 Sqn, Sayn-Wittgenstein's Ju 88C-6 was either mortally damaged by the rear gunner, Flt Lt Tom Thomson, or damaged by a Mosquito of No 141 Sqn flown by Flt Sgt Des Snape and Flg Off Ian Fowler. The latter subsequently reported;

'Flt Sgt Snape with Plt Off Fowler last off at 2125hrs, also to Brandenburg area. Target reached and patrolled until 2315hrs when a contact was obtained and chased. Mosquito closed in to about 200yds when a visual was obtained on an enemy aircraft, apparently a Ju 88 burning navigation lights. Flt Sgt Snape gave a 4/5 second burst but is making no claims pending assessment of cine film. Enemy aircraft opened fire in reply and our Mosquito was struck aft of cabin. No serious damage caused. No further contacts and aircraft turned for home landing, at 0120hrs.'

As no claim was made by the Mosquito crew, it is more likely that Flt Lt Tom Thomson was responsible for Sayn-Wittgenstein's demise. This is based on post-war research, when another survivor from the No 156 Sqn crew (all were taken prisoner), Flt Lt Alfred Muggeridge, recalled that they were attacked by a nightfighter, but on its second approach, the rear gunner held his fire until the range was very close. The Ju 88 was then seen to be hit and go down.

The nightfighter was riddled with gunfire, presumed to have come from below just as Sayn-Wittgenstein was about to fire a second burst into the Lancaster. He then dived away, ordered the cabin roof to be jettisoned and his crew (Feldwebel Friedrich Ostheimer and Unteroffizier Kurt Matzuleit) to bail out, which they did successfully. The following morning, the remains of the Ju 88C-6 and Major Heinrich *Prinz* zu Sayn-Wittgenstein's body were found near Lübars, east of Magdeburg. Two days later he was posthumously awarded the Swords to his Knight's Cross and Oak Leaves.

In this formal portrait, Major Heinrich *Prinz* zu Sayn-Wittgenstein is wearing his Knight's Cross (awarded to him in in October 1942 after he had shot down 22 aircraft all while flying the Ju 88C-6) and the Oak Leaves for this decoration (received in August 1943, by which time he was *Gruppenkommandeur* of II./NJG 3). In January 1944 Sayn-Wittgenstein took command of NJG 2, and later that month he was posthumously awarded the Swords to the Knight's Cross after having been killed in action on the night of the 20th. By then his tally had reached 83 victories (*Author's collection*)

APPENDICES

COLOUR PLATES COMMENTARY

1
Ju 88C-0 Wk-Nr 0096 CN+NR of Z.St./KG 30, Ludwigslust, Germany, spring 1940

This aircraft was the first prototype C-1 of a batch of 20. It, like the others, joined Z.St./KG 30 in April 1940, where the aircraft's Stammkennzeichen, CN+NR, was eventually replaced by 4D+OH at Ludwigslust on 10 July 1940. Its subsequent fate is unknown. Note that Wk-Nr 0096 has retained the nose Perspex glazing, albeit that on the starboard side has armour plating internally around the machine guns and cannon.

2
Ju 88C-2 G9+CM of 4./NJG 1, Düsseldorf, Germany, June 1940

Z.St./KG 30 moved to Düsseldorf in June 1940 in preparation for becoming a 4./NJG 1 – in September it was redesignated 1./NJG 2. A photograph of this aircraft and another coded G9+FM parked alongside a day camouflaged Ju 88C-1 of Z.St./KG 30 coded 4D+UZ (presumably Wk-Nr 0116) show them still retaining the KG 30 diving eagle, but just visible is the unit code G9 ahead of the fuselage cross, denoting their assignment to 4./NJG 1. It is unusual to note that the two 4./NJG 1 losses (Ju 88C-2 Wk-Nr 0126 4D+PZ on 5 July 1940 and Ju 88C-2 Wk-Nr 0245 4D+GZ on 17 August 1940) prior to it becoming 1./NJG 2 appear to have retained the Z.St./KG 30 codes.

3
Ju 88C-1 Wk-Nr 0142 4D+MH of Z.St./KG 40, Stavanger, Norway, June 1940

This aircraft, believed to have been flown by Unteroffizier Heinz Strüning, strayed too close to Swedish airspace on 7 June 1940 and was hit by anti-aircraft fire. Although the pilot duly carried out a successful force-landing at Bjørnfjell, near Narvik, Wk-Nr 0142 was so severely damaged that it was unrepairable. Strüning became a high-scoring intruder pilot over England in 1940–41, and he would ultimately receive the Knight's Cross with Oak Leaves on 20 July 1944. Eventually promoted to the rank of Hauptmann, Strüning, who had taken his victory tally to 56 (all at night), was killed in action while flying a Bf 110 with 9./NJG 1 on the night of 24 December 1944, shot down by a Mosquito of No 157 Sqn.

4
Ju 88C-4 Wk-Nr 0343 R4+CH of 1./NJG 2, Gilze-Rijen, the Netherlands, March 1941

This aircraft, flown by Oberleutnant Kurt Herrmann, took off from Gilze-Rijen on the night of 10 March 1941 to carry out an intruder mission over RAF airfields in East Anglia. However, it suffered double engine failure and was forced to crash-land near Terrington St Clement, in Norfolk, giving the RAF its first look at an intact Ju 88C. Herrmann had joined the Luftwaffe in 1934, having first flown with JG 134 in 1936 prior to becoming an instructor. Returning to operational flying with II./*Lehrgeschwader* (LG) 1 at Greifswald. He then joined Bf 110-equipped 2.(*Zerstörer*)/LG 1 in April 1938, flying with the unit until October 1939 – he claimed to have shot down two aircraft on 2 and 8 September over Poland. Promoted to Oberfeldwebel, Herrmann was then posted to *Luftkriegsschule* Fürstenfeldbruck from November 1939 until March 1940, when he joined Z.St./KG 30 (which ultimately became 1./NJG 2 in September 1940). He was the top-scoring *Fernnachtjagd* pilot at the time of his capture, with a total of nine victories.

5
Ju 88C-4 R4+MT of *Ergänzungs*/NJG 2, Gilze-Rijen, the Netherlands, spring 1942

III./NJG 2 was formed in March 1942, commanded by Hauptmann Herbert Bönsch. It initially operated a mixture of Ju 88C-2s and C-4s, prior to receiving its first Ju 88C-6. In October 1942, II./NJG 2 was formed from III./NJG 2, the original II./NJG 2 (flying Bf 110s and Do 215s) then becoming IV./NJG 1. Losses for III./NJG 2 were very light, with the first Ju 88C-6 to be destroyed in combat being Wk-Nr 360151 flown by Bönsch, who was shot down on the night of 31 July 1942. It appears that *Ergänzungs*/NJG 2 also used III. *Gruppe*-coded Ju 88s, with C-6 Wk-Nr 360178 R4+TR being lost in an accident on 28 March 1942. Likewise, Ju 88A-4 Wk-Nr 6139 R4+PR was lost in an accident on 17 April 1942. There was the occasional combat loss for *Ergänzungs*/NJG 2 too, with the first recorded example occurring on 17 February 1942 when Ju 88C-6 Wk-Nr 360153 R4+LR crashed returning from operations. On 31 May 1942, Ju 88C-4 Wk-Nr 630 R4+CT crashed at Gilze-Rijen, it probably being one of the 'Do 217s' claimed by Flt Sgt Colin Smith of Hurricane-equipped No 3 Sqn over the airfield that night. Profiled C-4 R4+MT was photographed after it force-landed some time in 1942, although the damage sustained was so minor that it appears not to have been recorded.

6
Ju 88C-4 R4+WK of 2./NJG 2, Benghazi, Libya, summer 1942

After intruder missions over Britain were stopped, I./NJG 2 began flying similar sorties over the Mediterranean at the start of November 1941, operating from both Catania and North African airfields. 2./NJG 2 was commanded by Oberleutnant Heinz Harmstorf until he was killed in action engaging a Wellington of No 40 Sqn on 22 July 1942. Having claimed 40 aircraft, I./NJG 2 was recalled to Belgium at the start of August 1942 and was soon in action against RAF Bomber Command. Note the partial white theatre band ahead of the tail on this aircraft.

7
Ju 88C-6 Wk-Nr 360219 R4+GT of 9./NJG 2, Gilze-Rijen, the Netherlands, September 1942

This aircraft, fitted with FuG 202 *Lichtenstein* BC AI radar and sporting 22 victory bars on its fin, was believed to have been flown by Oberfeldwebel Wilhelm Beier. The top-scoring intruder pilot flying with 3./NJG 2 in 1940–41, Beier was credited with 14 victories during this time, for which he was awarded the Knight's Cross in October 1941. It would appear that his earlier aircraft, Ju 88C-4 Wk-Nr 360351 R4+NL, was being flown by another ace, Leutnant Hans Hahn, on 11 October 1941 (the day after Beier's Knight's Cross was announced) when it collided with an Oxford trainer and crashed, the RAF finding a section of the tail marked with 13 kill bars within the wreckage of the Ju 88, this tally matching Beier's claims at the time. His 22nd victory came on 22 August 1942, and he would go on to shoot down a total of 37 aircraft and survive the war.

8
Ju 88C-6 Wk-Nr 360008 3U+KU of 10./ZG 26, Trapani, Sicily, April 1943

This aircraft differs from 3U+GU (see profile 17) in that it carries on its nose both the ZG 26 double rune badge and the rarely seen diving eagle of 10. *Staffel*. Wk-Nr 360008 crashed into the sea 50 km west of the island of Marettimo whilst being flown by Unteroffizier Hans Köhler, the aircraft having probably fallen victim to P-40 Warhawks of the 86th FS/79th FG. There were no survivors.

9

Ju 88C-6 F1+KR of 7./KG 76, Catania, Sicily, April 1943

Several bomber units operated the Ju 88C-6 in very small numbers, although why this was the case is not totally clear. One such *Kampfgeschwader* was KG 76, which reported losses of Ju 88C-6s over both the Russian Front and the Mediterranean while flying with *Stab*./KG 76, 2./KG 76, 4./KG 76, *Stab* III./KG 76 and 8./KG 76. III./KG 76 operated in the Mediterranean between November 1942 and July 1943, during which time it flew a maximum of five C-6s, although by mid-1943 it rarely had more than a single example on strength.

10

Ju 88C-6 5K+NT of 9.(*Eis*)/KG 3, Poltawa, Ukraine, April 1943

KG 3 started flying train-busting missions from mid-1942, although a specialist *Staffel* (9.(*Eis*)/KG 3) was not formed until January 1943. One of 9. *Staffel*'s first casualties was its *Staffelkapitän*, Hauptmann Otto Meichsner, although he was not flying a Ju 88C-6 when he was killed on 11 January. Meichsner was replaced by Oberleutnant Ernst Fach, who would be awarded the Knight's Cross posthumously following his death on 15 May. Leutnant Udo Cordes then took over, and he led the *Staffel* until it was withdrawn to Germany in June, when such train-busting missions with the Ju 88C-6 are believed to have ceased. Although not visible in this profile, 5K+NT, like all Ju 88C-6s of 9. *Staffel*, featured both KG 3's lightning marking and the wing and train wheel insignia similar to the badge of the *Deutsche Reichsbahn* (German National Railway).

11

Ju 88C-6 9K+HR of 7./KG 51, Bagerovo, Ukraine, spring 1943

III./KG 51 also operated a limited number of Ju 88C-6s in the train-busting role from August 1942 through to July 1943, the maximum establishment within the *Gruppe* being five. All three *Staffeln* reported C-6 losses during this time. In an attempt to confuse Soviet defences, the solid nose of a number of III. *Gruppe*'s C-6s (including 9K+HR depicted here) were painted to look like the Ju 88 as a standard A-variant bomber. 7. *Staffel* reported the loss of Wk-Nr 360324 9K+OR on 26 April 1943 and Wk-Nr 360172 9K+MR two days later – these were its only casualties in 11 months of combat. Not visible behind the port engine of this aircraft is the KG 51 Edelweiss insignia.

12

Ju 88C-6 F8+HX of 13./KG 40, Cognac, France, spring 1943

This aircraft, although camouflaged the same as F8+DY (see profile 14), has full-sized fuselage codes. The logbook of Unteroffizier Heinz Hommel records that it was regularly flown by him between 29 November 1942 and 31 July 1943. Oberleutnant Arthur Schröder's logbook records that he routinely flew F8+HX from 11 August to 21 September 1943.

13

Ju 88C-6 Wk-Nr 360063 F8+EZ of 15./KG 40, Lorient, France, spring 1943

This aircraft is believed to have been one of the original Ju 88C-6s assigned to V./KG 40, as those with similar Werk Nummer had either been destroyed or reassigned to IV./KG 40 (or other training units) by the summer of 1943. There is no record of this aircraft being damaged or lost while with V./KG 40 or I./ZG 1.

14

Ju 88C-6 F8+DY of 14./KG 40, Bordeaux-Mérignac, France, summer 1943

When V./KG 40 was formed in mid-1942, its Ju 88C-6s were camouflaged as if delivered from the factory. In mid-1943, they adopted the camouflage seen here, which appears in this case to have only been partially completed. Some of the 14./KG 40 aircraft also had wives' and girlfriends' names applied diagonally on the nose below the cockpit. For example, Oberleutnant Kurt Necesany's F8+RY featured the name of his fiancée, and later wife, Ruth.

15

Ju 88C-6 F8+MZ of 15./KG 40, Bordeaux-Mérignac, France, summer 1943

Photographs of this aircraft show it to have adopted another, slightly darker, camouflage compared to F8+DY. Annoyingly, V./KG 40 is inconsistent in the recording of losses or damage caused to its aircraft in 1943, so it is hard to find any further information on the history or fate of this aircraft.

16

Ju 88C-6 D5+EX of IV./NJG 3, Karup, Denmark, summer 1943

It has been stated in previous captions written to accompany photographs of this aircraft that it having the code +EX means it is a Ju 88C-6 of 13./NJG 2, but no evidence has ever emerged to support this. It is more likely that the aircraft is from IV./NJG 3, which was formed from 1. and 9./NJG 2 at Grove, in Denmark, in November 1942 and commanded by Major Erich Simon, formerly of III./NJG 2. He would eventually be shot down in combat on the night of 7 October 1943 while attacking a Stirling in Ju 88C-6 Wk-Nr 360372 D5+CF, his body later being washed ashore and buried at Esbjerg, in Denmark.

17

Ju 88C-6 Wk-Nr 750370 3U+GU of 10./ZG 26, Eleusis, Greece, August 1943

10./ZG 26 originally flew Do 17s over the Mediterranean in 1942 for daylight convoy escort duties. When I./NJG 2 departed the theatre, its Ju 88Cs were left behind for 10./ZG 26. On 25 August 1943, 3U+GU, flown by Leutnant Wilhelm Debes, collided with another Ju 88C flown by Unteroffizier Otto Müller and crashed into the sea off the island of Euboea, east of Athens. There were no survivors. That same month, half of 10./ZG 26 returned to Germany, with the remaining half becoming 11./ZG 26.

18

Ju 88C-6 F8+YZ of 15./KG 40, Bordeaux-Mérignac, France, autumn 1943

Sporting standard camouflage, this aircraft is also fitted with a FuG 227 *Flensburg* passive radar receiver, the aerial for which is visible under the port wing. F8+YZ was first flown by Oberfeldwebel Kurt Gäbler of 15./KG 40 on 29 August 1943, but it is not known if *Flensburg* was fitted at that time. Again, the full history, and fate, of this aircraft is not known.

19

Ju 88C-6 4C+AA of *Sonderkommando Kunkel*, Bordeaux-Mérignac, France, November 1943

Sonderkommando Kunkel, commanded by former Fw 200 pilot Hauptmann Fritz Kunkel, used Ju 88C-6s, Ju 88R-2s and at least one Ju 88G-1 equipped with the FuG 202 *Lichtenstein* and FuG 227 *Flensburg* AI radar against Allied aircraft over the Bay of Biscay at night and in bad weather. Drawing experienced crews from I. and III./ZG 1, the *Kommando* was officially formed on 15 January 1944, although Kunkel and his crew flew their first operation (a *Freie Jagd* to Cap Ortegal) on 12 November 1943, taking off from Bordeaux-Mérignac at 0308 hrs and landing at 0740 hrs.

20
Ju 88C-6 R4+KP of 6./NJG 2, Kassel-Rothwesten, Germany, May 1944
Despite the emergence of Ju 88Rs and Gs as nightfighters, II./NJG 2 was still operating Ju 88C-6s in May 1944, as was III./NJG 2 which reported an accident involving Ju 88C-6 Wk-Nr 750692 R4+NR of 7. *Staffel* on the 19th. Even I./NJG 2 had a number on strength, reporting the loss in combat of Ju 88C-6 Wk-Nr 750954 of 2. *Staffel* on 10 June. However, by July, I./NJG 2 only had Ju 88G-1s, likewise II. *Gruppe*. III./NJG 2 had its last Ju 88C-6s replaced by Ju 88G-1s and G-6s in August.

BIBLIOGRAPHY

Balss, Michael, *Deutsche Nachtjagd*, Stefan Kehl (1997)

Boiten, Theo, *Nachtjagd War Diaries Volume 1*, Wing Leader (2011)

Chorley, W R, *Royal Air Force Bomber Command Losses of the Second World War Vol 3–5*, Midland Counties (1994–97)

Foreman, John, *RAF Fighter Command Victory Claims of World War 2 – Part 2 1941–1943*, Red Kite (2005)

Franks, Norman, *Conflict over the Bay*, Grub Street (1986)

Goss, Chris, *Bloody Biscay*, Crécy (1997)

Goss, Chris, *Luftwaffe Intruder Operations over the United Kingdom*, Pen & Sword (2025)

Goss, Chris, *Sea Eagles Volumes 1 and 2*, Classic (2006)

Goss, Chris and Streetly, Martin, *Junkers Ju 88 Day and Nightfighters*, Classic (2023)

Kaiser, Jochen, *Der Ritterkreuzträger der Kampfflieger Band 1 and Band 2*, Luftfahrtverlag-Start (2010)

Obermaier, Ernst, *Die Ritterkreuzträger der Luftwaffe 1939–1945 – Band I* Jagdflieger, Verlag Dieter Hoffmann (1989)

Parry, Simon, *Intruders over Britain*, Air Research Publications (1987)

Patzwall, Klaus, *Der Ehrenpokal für besondere Leistungen im Luftkrieg*, Verlag Patzwall (2008)

Rökker, Heinz, *Chronik I. Gruppe Nachtjagdgeschwader 2*, VDM (1997)

Scherzer, Veit, *Die Träger Des Deutschen Kreuzes in Gold der Luftwaffe 1941–1945*, Scherzer Verlag (1992)

Parker, Nigel, *Luftwaffe Crash Archive Volumes 9–12*, Wing Leader (2016–18)

Shores, Christopher, *Fledgling Eagles*, Grub Street (1991)

INDEX